# Alternatives to ALCOHOL ABUSE

## A Social Learning Model

# Peter M. Miller · Marie A. Mastria

**Research Press Company**

2612 North Mattis Avenue • Champaign, Illinois 61820

ISBN 0-87822-133-6
Library of Congress Catalog Card Number 76-52356

*To our parents,*
*Purdy and Alice Miller*
*Ernest and Rose Mastria*

# Contents

# Preface

With approximately 9 million alcoholics in the United States, the number of alcoholism counselors is growing rapidly. Concomitantly, the need for continuing education of those going into the field is great. In response to this need, several colleges and universities have established alcoholism counselor training programs for individuals with little previous formal training. In addition, institutions of higher learning are developing specialties in alcoholism treatment for professional trainees (e.g., clinical psychologists). Recent national efforts to certify alcoholism counselors have been aimed at formalizing adequate training opportunities.

This book represents a practical therapy manual that can be used as an adjunct to such training. It is aimed at therapists and counselors who are treating alcoholics in mental health centers, hospitals, alcoholism treatment centers, and half-way houses. The book is a basic "how-to-do-it" handbook that does not require sophisticated knowledge of psychological theory or treatment.

Social learning is the general orientation of the approach presented in the book. Treatment techniques based on learning principles are of growing interest not only in the field of alcoholism but also in the whole area of mental health. These techniques offer the alcoholism counselor a structured, problem-oriented approach to clients.

# Acknowledgments

The authors wish to thank Mary Plunkett, Linda McGee, Marcia Rodgers, and Linda Wilbanks for typing the manuscript. Dr. Mastria wishes to thank Angela Howell for her comments on various chapters. The editorial assistance of Ann Music Streetman and Ann Wendel was greatly appreciated by both authors.

# 1 Alcohol Abuse: A Functional Analysis

## THEORIES AND TREATMENT STRATEGIES

Various treatment approaches are available in the alcoholism field, including "fads" based upon the current popularity of particular techniques. These widely varying methods include individual and group therapy, psychodrama, milieu therapy, transactional analysis, aversion conditioning, community abstinence groups, and medications, such as tranquilizers, antidepressants, LSD, and disulfiram (Antabuse). The question of which treatment procedure to use is quite dismaying to the counselor, particularly when proponents of each approach claim theirs to be the best or even the *only* effective method of treatment. Unfortunately, few of the advocates of these treatments bother to objectively report the effectiveness of their methods as assessed by well controlled treatment evaluation studies.

Part of the confusion over treatment methods lies in the fact that, at present, no *one* theory satisfactorily explains the development and maintenance of chronic heavy drinking. A number of alternative explanations of alcoholism exist. These various explanations have in turn suggested different treatment. Some "experts" claim that alcoholism is mainly a function of sociocultural variables and that treatment-prevention strategies should involve environmental engineering and mass attitude change techniques. Others claim that alcoholism is a physical disease related to such factors as nutritional deficiencies or hereditary influences. Still others claim that abusive drinking is caused by personality defects, such as self-destructive impulses, "oral" dependency needs, or an extreme need for power and autonomy. Thus, they espouse long-term psychotherapy. Unfortunately, there is conflicting evidence which both supports and refutes these theories.

The varied explanations of alcoholism and their related treatments leave the counselor in a dilemma. Which treatment techniques are the most useful and effective? Frequently, in searching for the

1

answer to this question through "summer schools," conferences, and workshops, the counselor becomes even more confused. More times than not, the information she obtains at these meetings seems irrelevant to the day-to-day counseling of alcoholic individuals. Even when treatment is covered, it is often done in vague discussions of the alcoholic's manipulative behavior or dependency with very few concrete suggestions offered.

This book describes a new practical approach to alcoholism counseling. It is based upon a functional analysis of *problems in living,* not on any one theoretical framework. It assumes that, on the basis of our current knowledge, no one theory of alcoholism is satisfactory and that alcohol abuse is probably related to numerous sociological, physiological, and psychological factors. It further assumes that treatment techniques should be derived from the current problems of the alcoholic, not from a particular theoretical frame of reference. In other words, we *cannot* and *need not wait* for all the answers to why people become alcoholics before we establish effective treatments. Prevention, of course, may rely more heavily on such information.

## SOCIAL VERSUS PROBLEM DRINKERS
Before discussing the specifics of this treatment approach, we must spend some time on the definition of our problem. Fully 90 percent of adults who drink alcohol do so in a moderate, controlled manner. Although an individual may have "one too many" on an occasional basis, most drinkers do not habitually abuse alcohol. One out of every 10 alcohol users, however, does become a problem drinker. That is, he drinks too much, too often. The difference between a heavy drinker, a problem drinker, and an alcoholic is often questioned. Professionals and laymen alike have turned these distinctions into a very complicated issue. Each "expert" seems to have his own classification system based on various "symptoms" (e.g., early morning drinking, increased tolerance for alcohol, secretive drinking, etc.).

Labeling persons on the basis of these symptoms serves no useful purpose, especially in terms of telling the counselor what to do to help someone who drinks too much. In this book we will view alcohol use and abuse along a continuum. In terms of the frequency of alcohol use on a daily or weekly basis, people vary from complete abstinence to heavy daily drinking. There is no magical point on this continuum at which an individual becomes an "alcoholic."

Because of differences in individual tolerance levels for alcohol, we cannot base problem drinking on *how much* someone drinks. Rather, we usually think of problem drinking in terms of the *effects* of

2

alcohol on daily life functioning. Within this framework, an individual has a drinking problem if he *habitually* has life problems after drinking episodes. The frequency of these occurrences indicates the seriousness of the problem.

Some persons appear to be able to drink quite heavily every day without experiencing significant problems in living. That is, they continue to function well in their marriage, their job, and with their friends. However, alcohol is a drug which is physically addictive. The heavy drinker who shows no obvious outward signs of dysfunction may be developing serious medical problems which may be discovered only after years of heavy drinking.

A more relevant issue, however, is that a chronic, heavy user of alcohol may not be able to maintain a stable level of alcohol consumption over time. The nature of alcohol itself makes it likely that some persons will develop drug tolerance. **Tolerance** refers to the fact that a person gradually needs more and more alcohol to attain the same "high" that he once received from lower doses. Thus, alcohol itself forces him to become more and more dependent on its use. The eventual result is physical addiction. Once an individual becomes physically addicted, he must continue to drink or else experience unpleasant withdrawal symptoms.

In some cases a heavy drinker does not realize the extent of his dependence on alcohol until he is forced to do without it. For example, a 45-year-old man who is addicted may enter the hospital for surgery and be surprised that by the second day he begins to experience agitation, anxiety, sweating, and heart palpitations. By the third day, if he has not received medication to combat these symptoms, he may begin to hallucinate, seeing snakes crawling up the walls of his hospital room or roaches crawling over his body. Such experiences are part of the syndrome known as DT's or **delirium tremens**. This syndrome and the other discomforts the man has experienced are classical symptoms of alcohol withdrawal. In most cases, however, an individual's drinking problem becomes noticeable to others long before physical addiction occurs.

Generally, then, we think of problem drinking in terms of (1) the effects that alcohol has on an individual's social, emotional, physiological, occupational, or marital functioning on any occasion together with (2) the frequency of occurrence of these incidents. Alcohol consumption *consistently has a negative influence* on the life of a problem drinker and on the lives of others around him.

The task of those who treat the problem drinker is *not* to diagnose his alcoholism on the basis of "symptoms." Rather, it is to recognize and attempt to deal with the alcoholic's *life problems* associated with the consumption of alcohol (i.e., problems can be either precipitants of drinking or the results of it). Using this view of alcoholism differs from employing the traditional disease model in which inordinate amounts of time are spent convincing the client to admit that he is an alcoholic because of certain symptoms. Although using the disease model is often helpful in bringing a problem drinker into treatment, it focuses away from the real life problems with which he must deal. Also, thinking of clients as "alcoholics!" presupposes that they are all very much alike and that treatment should be similar for all. This is simply not true. Therefore, counseling must be individualized and focus on all the client's problems, with alcohol abuse being only one of them.

## DEFINING THE FUNCTIONAL-PRACTICAL APPROACH

Basically, this new treatment approach is based upon a social-learning model in which alcohol abuse is viewed as a socially acquired (*learned*) behavior pattern maintained by numerous antecedent and consequent events. *That is, therapeutic intervention is based upon the specific factors in an individual's life that either occur soon before excessive drinking begins (antecedents) or soon after it has been initiated (consequences).* The antecedent and consequent events may be psychological, physiological, or sociological. Such general factors as reduction in unpleasant emotional or cognitive states (i.e., anxiety, boredom), increase of peer approval, ability to exhibit more varied, spontaneous interpersonal behavior, or avoidance of physiological withdrawal symptoms may maintain alcohol abuse.

We place the major emphasis of our assessment and intervention on events that are *currently* associated with heavy drinking. These events are sometimes called **maintaining factors**. Thus, when we talk about what causes an individual to drink too much, we are referring to these maintaining events. This emphasis makes it easier to do something about the problem. The notion differs from the typical way clinical problems are depicted, particularly within a psychiatric frame of reference. Traditionally, causation is described in terms of personality or environmental factors that initially predisposed an individual to use alcohol inappropriately. These we refer to as **precipitating factors** or causes. Although such causes are intriguing from a developmental or preventive point of view, they do not often contribute meaningfully to the treatment process. The reason is that the factors which *originally* caused an individual to drink too much may no longer be related to current excessive drinking. Miller and Eisler have described this discrepancy between precipitating and maintaining causes in the context of the following case.[1] Suppose that a young housewife experiencing marital problems begins to drink excessively to relieve her tension and worry over her marriage. Her drinking continues, the marital problem worsens, and she and her husband obtain a divorce. She continues to drink too much in response to emotionally stressful situations. When she is intoxicated, her anxiety is reduced and she escapes psychologically from stressful circumstances. Her drinking gradually increases in frequency so that she is drinking daily. Early morning drinking relieves agitation and hangover from the previous evening drinking bout. As her life deteriorates, she loses contact with friends who might serve as positive influences on her. Association with these friends tends to lead to thoughts of guilt and embarrassment that lead to more drinking. She then begins to associate exclusively with alcoholic men and women. At this point, the original *precipitating factor* of marital stress is no longer present. There would be little purpose in describing the cause of this woman's drinking as her inability to find viable solutions to a marital problem. Her drinking continues, at present, for *maintaining reasons,* such as peer encouragement and approval, feelings of guilt over her present lifestyle, and the avoidance of withdrawal symptoms. Treatment must focus on these current maintaining factors since they are the most potent influences on her drinking. Once these influences are modified and her drinking is terminated, then, and only then, would counseling efforts designed to teach her to handle interpersonal stress be appropriate. At that point, they would decrease the likelihood of relapse.

## ASSESSING ANTECEDENT AND CONSEQUENT EVENTS

As indicated earlier, the categories of possible antecedent and consequent events related to excessive drinking are numerous. They include *emotional, social, cognitive, situational,* and *physiological* events. Figure 1 illustrates the relationship of alcohol abuse to these antecedent and consequent events.

We assume that abusive drinking not only occurs in response to these cues (events) but that it also modifies the environment to bring about certain (often desirable) ends. Thus, in an attempt to cope with social, emotional, situational, cognitive, and physiological situations, the problem drinker's first response is to consume alcohol. She might do this because of basic deficiencies in coping skills, i.e., she does not know how to handle the situation, except through drinking. In addition, she may experience intense anxiety which prevents an appropriate response. On a short-term basis, abusive drinking serves as an adjustment mechanism. That is, it is a definite response which functions to change (and often temporarily improve) a problem situation. Drinking,

*FIGURE 1.    FUNCTIONAL ANALYSIS OF ALCOHOL ABUSE*

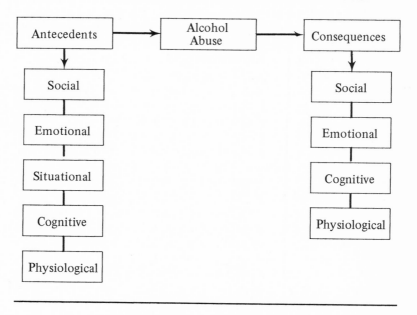

then, can result in positive consequences in relation to the initial antecedent event which precipitated it. An example follows.

In the presence of her co-workers Joan is berated by one of her supervisors for doing unsatisfactory work. Actually, her work has been rated fine by other supervisors. The supervisor who criticized her is a rather unpleasant person who seems to delight in making other people feel uncomfortable. After the incident, Joan feels very hurt and angry. She thinks that she should do something about the situation but is not sure what to do. She has always had difficulty in confronting people with her feelings. Her inability to confront the supervisor makes her feel even worse about herself.

As a result of this situation, Joan goes home that evening and drinks heavily. The immediate effects of her drinking are positive in that she (1) feels less angry and upset, (2) worries less and develops an "I-don't-care" attitude, and (3) begins to think more positively about herself. She might even decide to confront the supervisor by calling him on the phone and cursing him. Again, this gives her a feeling of satisfaction. Thus, the *immediate* consequences of her heavy drinking are positive. Psychological studies of learning tell us that our behavior is very much effected by its *immediate* or *short-term* consequences. That is, if our behavior works, if it improves a situation or enables us to cope more effectively, we tend to repeat that behavior under similar circumstances. We are much less influenced by long-term consequences of our behavior.

For example, on the morning after her drinking episode, Joan may experience a number of problems. In addition to an agonizing hangover, she may (1) feel upset and worried over getting drunk, (2) worry about the consequences of her intoxicated behavior, and (3) begin to think more negatively about herself. Also, when she returns to work, she may experience more problems with her supervisor than she had before as a result of her *aggressive,* as opposed to *assertive*, telephone confrontation. While alcohol had enabled her to react to the supervisor, she actually overreacted and demonstrated very poor judgment. In the long run, her drinking actually made the situation worse. This state of affairs typically leads to more drinking in an attempt to cope with an increasing number of problems. Joan might continue to drink heavily in a frustrated attempt to solve her problems or to escape from them.

To further analyze the impact of these factors in general, we will present a more detailed picture of some of the possible social-environmental events related to excessive drinking. Tables 1 and 2 describe several specific antecedent and consequent events in the categories of social, emotional, situational, cognitive, and physiological factors.

## Social Factors

Recent studies at Rutgers University, Baltimore City Hospitals, and the University of Washington indicate that specific interpersonal situations may regularly precede, and hence, precipitate excessive drinking episodes in alcohol abusers. Boredom or social isolation often set the occasion for heavy drinking. An individual may drink to relieve boredom or to provide self-stimulation in an otherwise drab psychological existence.

Alcoholics may drink also in relation to interpersonal conflict and stress. In this case, alcohol consumption often leads to an enhanced ability to exhibit more varied and spontaneous social behavior. The shy, passive individual finds that, after a few drinks, he is more talkative and vivacious. In turn, others may respond more positively toward him when he behaves this way. Generally, social interactions tend to be more satisfying to alcoholics after alcohol consumption.

Social interactions may affect drinking habits even more directly through modeling and group pressure. Simply stated, **modeling** refers to the psychological phenomenon that persons tend to behave as those around them. Thus, an individual exposed to friends or acquaintances who heavily use alcohol may begin to imitate them (without being aware of it) by drinking more heavily. Essentially, this is learning by example. This indicates that the drinking habits of the group which one associates with are extremely important to one's own drinking. In addition, there is often a tendency for friends, especially at a social event, to encourage the problem drinker to "have one more for the road." Dr. Alan Marlatt at the University of Washington recently found that social pressure from friends is one of the major precipitants of relapse in alcoholics.[2] "Friends" often go out of their way to entice a problem drinker who is currently sober to begin drinking again. Once drinking begins, these "friends" provide a significant amount of support, attention, and encouragement for drinking. These positive consequences of drinking set up a pattern which helps to maintain excessive drinking over time.

Even though some short-term social consequences of drinking are positive, drinking can and eventually does lead to decreased ability to function interpersonally. Although the shy, inhibited person may begin to loosen up after three or four drinks, she may become overbearing and hostile after six or seven. In addition, excessive drinking can lead to withdrawal of attention by others repulsed by drunken behavior. An intoxicated individual, however, can usually obtain a response from someone, even if she must force it. For many alchoholics, a negative response (e.g., threats and lectures) can do as much to maintain their drinking as a positive response. As we will describe later, one of the treatment goals is to arrange for a more consistent set of social consequences for drinking.

## Emotional Factors

The relationship between unpleasant emotional states—anxiety and stress—and excessive alcohol consumption has long been considered important. Supposedly, alcohol serves to reduce tension and anxiety, leading to a more pleasant emotional state or at least relief from an unpleasant one.

Recent evidence suggests that this relationship is not as simple as it once appeared. For example, some studies indicate that chronic alcoholics actually experience *increases* in anxiety and depression subsequent to drinking. It appears that their drinking is not a function of tension reduction *per se*. Nonalcoholic social drinkers exhibit quite a different pattern as they drink moderately. After small amounts of alcohol, social drinkers do report *decreases* in anxiety and increases in positive, relaxed feelings. As they consume more alcohol, however, they begin to experience the same anxiety and depression reported by chronic alcoholics. It may be that while tension reduction can serve as an important factor in the beginning of an individual's alcohol abuse, it becomes less important with chronicity. Therefore, therapeutic attempts to help chronic alcoholics relieve anxiety may be inappropriate with many clients. Although this intervention may have been useful earlier in a person's drinking history, the counselor must now aim treatment at other maintaining causes.

General emotional arousal also can be involved in excessive drinking. Studies have shown that the tranquilizing effects of alcohol are more potent under conditions of emotional arousal (either negative or positive arousal). This might account for many alcoholics reporting that they began a drinking binge, not when they were having problems, but when they felt exhilarated because "things were going so well."

In any event, the relationship between stress and drinking is very complex. The exact relationship seems to be related to personality characteristics of the individual, the type of stress, and the context in which stress occurs. For example, there is some evidence that interpersonal situations requiring assertiveness (the ability to effectively express either positive or negative feelings) are particularly stressful for alcoholics, frequently leading to excessive drinking. Some other kind of interpersonal stress may not be as strongly associated with drinking. In situations requiring assertiveness, alcohol often enables the alcoholic to respond more openly. Often, however, this response is overreactive so that the individual becomes hostile or overly sensitive. When a person is extremely angry, alcohol consumption can also dissipate the anger and lead to an "I-don't-care" attitude.

In counseling, then, the influence of stress as a maintaining cause must be evaluated on a case-by-case basis. One can never assume that tension reduction is a factor in drinking until a full assessment of the client is completed. Even if the counselor did determine that anxiety serves as a precipitant to heavy drinking, this general information alone would not be very helpful in treatment. The nature of specific anxiety-producing situations which precede drinking must be determined.

## Situational Factors

From studies of learning, we know that persons learn certain patterns of behavior through repeated associations between events occurring in their environment. After repeated associations between eating snacks while watching a certain television program, the television program may begin to serve as an external hunger cue. In the same manner, beer advertisements may initiate certain thoughts and feelings ("cravings") about having a drink. Situational factors associated with, and eventually leading to, alcohol abuse do not have to be alcohol-related. An individual's drinking can become associated with time factors. Thus, at 5 p.m. every day she has a strong desire for a drink mainly because drinking has occurred so frequently at this time. Specific persons, places, and situations also can serve this cue function. In terms of counseling, these cues must be determined so that the problem drinker initially can change her schedule to avoid them, thus decreasing the likelihood of drinking. An individual can schedule other activities during times in which she is most likely to drink. Techniques to help an individual accomplish this goal will be discussed in Chapter 8.

## Cognitive Factors

Oddly enough, there is less known about cognitive factors that lead to excessive drinking than about any other influence on alcohol abuse. However, there has probably been more written on these factors than any others. This means that there are a number of theories which take into account the alcoholic's thought patterns as they relate to drinking. Since we cannot directly observe or measure "thought," it is very difficult to prove or disprove these theories. From a clinical standpoint, however, many alcoholics report that their drinking is precipitated by negative thoughts about themselves ("I'm just no damn good!"), retaliatory thoughts ("I'll show her who's boss!"), or guilt-related thoughts ("I shouldn't have taken my anger out on the children"). Excessive drinking frequently changes these thoughts to more positive ones or at least provides an anesthetic to block out the thought.

## Physiological Factors

From a physical standpoint, drinking can be seen as an attempt to lessen pain and physical discomfort. Many problem drinkers report that alcohol consumption relieves headaches, backaches, etc. More permanent relief of the pain through medical treatment might be indicated as part of the total alcoholism treatment. Psychological techniques to help an individual live with chronic and medically untreatable discomfort are available and easily can be taught to the client.

Drinking can be related also to the alleviation of withdrawal symptoms. If someone who has been drinking heavily attempts to stop drinking, unpleasant physical withdrawal symptoms may serve as a cue for continued drinking. That is, the person avoids withdrawal symptoms by continuing to drink. It appears alcoholics can drink to maintain certain blood/alcohol levels that are maximally satisfying and least likely to cause withdrawal. Studies have even indicated that a decreasing blood/alcohol level often initiates further drinking in a chronic alcoholic.

---

TABLE 1. *POSSIBLE ANTECEDENTS (PRECIPITANTS) OF ALCOHOL ABUSE*

| *Factors* | *Antecedent Events* |
|---|---|
| Social | 1. Social isolation (boredom)<br>2. Interpersonal conflict and stress<br>3. Positive interpersonal situations requiring behaviors in which the individual is deficient (e.g., adequate sexual functioning)<br>4. Heavy drinking friends (modeling influences)<br>5. Group pressure to drink |
| Emotional | 1. Unpleasant feelings (anxiety, anger, depression), especially when combined with inability to express them<br>2. Heightened emotional arousal (either positive or negative) |
| Situational | 1. Observing alcohol advertisements<br>2. Passing by a bar<br>3. Observing others drinking<br>4. Hearing references to drinking |
| Cognitive | 1. Negative self-reference thoughts<br>2. Retaliatory thoughts (e.g., "I'll show her!")<br>3. Guilt-related thoughts |
| Physiological | 1. Pain or physical discomfort<br>2. Decreases in blood/alcohol level<br>3. Withdrawal symptoms |

---

TABLE 2. *POSSIBLE CONSEQUENCES OF ALCOHOL ABUSE*

| Factors | Positive Consequences | Negative Consequences |
|---|---|---|
| Social | 1. Enhanced behavioral repertoire<br>2. Attention and encouragement from friends | 1. Decreased behavioral functioning<br>2. Confrontation or withdrawal of attention by others |
| Emotional | 1. Enhanced ability to express feelings<br>2. Decreases in anxiety, boredom, depression, worry | 1. Tendency to overreact emotionally (overly sensitive, hostile)<br>2. Increases in anxiety and depression |
| Cognitive | 1. Increases in positive self-reference thoughts<br>2. Decreases in negative self-reference thoughts | 1. Increases in negative self-reference or guilt-related thoughts |
| Physiological | 1. Decreases in pain and physical discomfort<br>2. Decreases in withdrawal symptoms | 1. Increased possibility of physical withdrawal symptoms and chronic physical disabilities (e.g., cirrhosis of the liver) |

## THERAPEUTIC GOALS

Analyzing abusive drinking in relation to each of these factors involving antecedent and consequent events allows the counselor to establish specific therapeutic goals for the client. Based upon a functional analysis of these factors, intervention would involve:

1. Altering *antecedent conditions* so that they are less likely to elicit drinking behavior.
2. Altering *consequent conditions* so that they are less likely to maintain drinking behavior.
3. Teaching the client alternative ways of coping with people, places, situations, and feelings associated with heavy drinking.

More specifically in relation to these goals, the counselor might:

1. Assist the client in socializing only with non-drinkers (i.e., modification of a social-situational antecedent).

2. Arrange for relatives to provide attention and recognition for sobriety and withdrawal of all interaction for abusive drinking (i.e., modification of a social consequence).
3. Teach the client through role playing, behavioral rehearsal, and videotape feedback more effective ways of handling anger-provoking situations (i.e., modification of the client's response to a social-emotional antecedent).

The exact manner in which the client's drinking is assessed and goals are established will be discussed in Chapters 2 and 3. Suffice it to say here that this *functional approach involves an explicit statement of both goals and therapeutic procedures.* Of the goals mentioned, this book will concentrate on teaching the alcoholic better ways of adjusting her environment. Although rearranging antecedent and consequent events is very important, the counselor frequently has limited access to the client's environment. Thus, it is often difficult, if not impossible, to involve friends, relatives, or employers in treatment. This is not essential, however, since there are counseling techniques that teach the client to rearrange her own social-situational environment. Emphasis on teaching the client to manage her own environment (in a sense, to plan and implement her own modification in antecedent and consequent events) often provides the client with an enhanced self-concept. That is, the client learns how to better herself and those around her. This is a key point since traditional alcoholism treatment has been geared too often toward the counselor or **significant other** (person important to the client) doing something to the alcoholic to change her. As persons experienced in counseling alcholics know, the traditional treatment often leads to increased defensiveness and resistance to change on the client's part. In the functional therapeutic system, the client is expressly involved in both setting goals and establishing and implementing the treatment plan.

## THERAPEUTIC TECHNIQUES

A variety of specific therapeutic intervention strategies are available to teach problem drinkers alternatives to alcohol abuse. The techniques that will be discussed throughout this book are listed below:
1. relaxation training
2. assertion training
3. social- and marital-skills training
4. self-control training
5. occupational-skills training
6. sexual-relationships training

Using these techniques, counselors can teach clients skills that will enable these alcoholic clients to achieve self-management and thus to cope with life more effectively.

**Relaxation training** is a procedure that teaches a person how to initiate complete muscular and cognitive relaxation. The technique provides a way of dealing with anxiety and tension or cravings to take a drink. **Assertion training** consists of teaching the client to directly express personal rights and feelings (both positive and negative). This training is very structured. It includes role playing interpersonal situations similar to ones in the client's life by means of instructions, personal and videotape feedback, modeling (providing an example of an effective response), and behavioral rehearsal (i.e., practice). Clients are taught appropriate ways of expressing feelings. The goal is not to teach sarcasm or hostility, but assertiveness. In fact, assertion training is used not only for passive, inhibited individuals but also for those who are *too* expressive with their feelings in terms of hostility or emotional outbursts.

In the same manner, social and marital skills are taught through a structured role-playing approach. Clients might be taught how to initiate friendships (as an alternative to boredom), how to maintain mutually satisfying relationships, how to effectively solve marital disagreements, or how to provide more satisfactions to marital partners.

Self-control skills involve behavior patterns that help the client control and manage his own environment. In this sense, he serves as his own counselor. Thus, the client might be taught ways to schedule incompatible activities (e.g., playing with the children, or eating a meal) at times when drinking is most likely. He also might be taught how to reschedule consequences to reward himself for sobriety. The ability to give ourselves a "pat on the back" seems important in maintaining new behavior patterns. Self-control also involves cognitive retraining, which is akin to Dr. Albert Ellis's rational emotive therapy.[3] Thus, the counselor analyzes what the client is thinking (i.e., what he is saying to himself) and suggests changes. For example, the counselor might have him practice thinking positive thoughts about himself. This is often a new experience for problem drinkers! The client also might learn to question some of his illogical thoughts, such as "She doesn't like me. Therefore, I must be no good."

Occupational- and recreational-skills training provides extremely important alternatives to excessive drinking although its importance is often minimized by counselors. The counselor often takes it for granted that someone has the necessary skills to interview for a job, get along with co-workers, or structure spare-time activities. These skills can be taught in the same way that other coping skills are taught.

## ADVANTAGES OF THE FUNCTIONAL APPROACH

Several advantages accrue from using the functional treatment model that has been described. *First,* this approach stresses setting specific treatment goals. Both the counselor and client can be involved actively in goal setting. Establishing goals in this manner allows the client and counselor to continuously evaluate progress. Therapeutic success does not rely on some arbitrary criterion, such as one year of abstinence, but on day-to-day, problem-oriented coping skills. These skills can be assessed along a continuum so that small improvements can be recognized. Thus, if an emotionally inhibited client is able to respond more affectionately toward a loved one, one bit of success has been achieved. Assessing a client's progress in this way prevents the marked frustration and pessimism often inherent in working with alcoholics over time. A counselor may see no progress at all if she measures success only in terms of a specified period of abstinence. Emphasizing and recognizing the smaller steps that go into making sobriety work provides a more positive attitude for both counselor and client and a more effective therapeutic relationship.

*Second,* by establishing an explicit strategy of treatment, the counselor readily can determine specific intervention procedures and begin to see more clearly what works and what does not work. Therapists often criticize this approach for being too structured and too mechanical. Certainly, the functional model removes much of the mystique from the counseling relationship. However, this type of direct analysis and treatment of alcohol problems does *not* imply that the relationship aspects of counseling are omitted. As with any approach to clinical problems, the client must learn to have faith in the counselor. No counseling endeavor would be successful without adequate rapport between both parties. In fact, the counselor often must use the "inter-personal-emotional" influence that has developed from the counseling relationship to encourage and maintain behavior changes in the client.

*Third,* this therapeutic model facilitates the objective evaluation of counseling effectiveness. Since goals and treatments are so specific, it is relatively easy to set up a system to evaluate them. Effectiveness of treatment becomes individualized since each client's improvement is being measured against her own level of functioning at the initiation of counseling. This scientific-evaluative model also will help to eventually weed out ineffective treatments and to develop new, more effective ones.

## OUTLINE OF THE BOOK

This book is designed to teach you, as a therapist or counselor of alcoholic individuals, specific therapeutic techniques designed to provide the problem drinker with alternatives to alcohol abuse. These techniques assume a social-learning, functional explanation of abusive drinking, and for the most part, are based upon well founded clinical-experimental data on their effectiveness.

In essence, this is a "how-to-do-it" manual. Specific methods of assessing the client's problems and establishing a treatment plan will be discussed. Readers will be provided with a step-by-step description of how to implement various treatment strategies and some of the problems inherent in their use. Questions of both initiating and maintaining new modes of adjustment will be addressed.

## *Footnotes*

1. P. M. Miller and R. M. Eisler. Alcohol and drug abuse. In W. E. Craighead, A. E. Kazdin, and M. J. Mahoney, eds., *Behavior modification principles, issues, and applications.* Boston: Houghton Mifflin, 1976, 376-393.

2. G. A. Marlatt. A comparison of aversive conditioning procedures in the treatment of alcoholism. Paper presented at the Western Psychological Association, April, 1973.

3. A. Ellis. *Reason and emotion in psychotherapy.* New York: Lyle-Stuart, 1962.

# 2 Assessment of the Client's Problems

One of the most essential elements of counseling within a social-learning frame of reference is a detailed assessment of the client's problems. Baseline data provide the basis on which the counselor (1) establishes therapeutic goals, (2) formulates a treatment plan, and (3) evaluates the effectiveness of her intervention with the client. Unfortunately, many counselors perform a very cursory assessment of their clients, placing greatest emphasis on drinking behavior *per se*. Assessment must be multifaceted and should include not only information on drinking but also data on social, emotional, marital, cognitive, and vocational functioning.

Thus, the first few counseling sessions would comprise (1) general information gathering, (2) assessment of the client's immediate needs, (3) assessment of past and present alcohol abuse, (4) assessment of social and marital behaviors, (5) assessment of social-psychological functioning, and (6) assessment of vocational and recreational behaviors.

## INITIAL CLIENT INTERVIEW

The initial client contact is important in setting the tone for future counseling sessions. Whenever possible, this session should focus on establishing rapport with the client with only minimal data gathering. Extensive information gathering at this first visit often will alienate the client and lessen the likelihood that he will return (or, in an inpatient setting, that he will cooperate with treatment). Generally, the initial session should be spent in identifying the client's *immediate* problems and concerns, establishing rapport, and providing a positive treatment outcome expectancy.

The following two transcripts illustrate an ineffective and an effective method of initiating a counseling relationship. Note the approach of Counselor No. 1.

17

## INEFFECTIVE

| Counselor | Client |
|---|---|
| Why did you come here? | My wife says that I drink too much. |
| Did you come because you really wanted to, or because your wife made you come? | I guess a little of both. |
| You must recognize your alcoholism and want to change, or we will not be able to help you. | I understand that. |
| Are you an alcoholic? | I'm not sure. I don't think so. (*Somewhat defensive*) |
| You are avoiding your problem. You must admit that you are an alcoholic before we can treat you. | I know that I have a problem . . . that I drink too much . . . but I don't need a drink every day. |
| How often and how much do you drink? | I drink about as much as other people that I know. I overdo it and get drunk about twice a week. |
| And you still say that you're not an alcoholic? | I told you that I don't think so! (*Becoming angry*) |
| Why do you get so angry when I ask you about your drinking? | I'm not angry! |
| You sure sound that way to me. You must be honest with me, or I can't help you. | (*Silence*) |
| Your motivation to change seems very poor. I'm not certain that we can help you unless you change your attitude. | (*Silence, looking angry*) |
| I have to fill out some forms on you. What is your full name? | John Baker Smith. |
| How old are you? | 39. |
| Where do you work? | I'm self-employed. |

The counselor continued asking a number of specific questions. The client continued to be defensive and angry and was seriously considering never returning to the treatment agency again. The counselor spent most of this session challenging and confronting the client about his motivation for treatment. Attempts to *convince* the client that he is an alcoholic are usually doomed. Although confrontation often is necessary in counseling, it must occur within the context of a positive relationship between the counselor and client.

Emphasis should be placed on *positive* aspects of the client's behavior. For example, the client did come to the treatment facility and did admit to some problems with alcohol. With an abrupt manner, the counselor in the above case essentially punished the client for both of these positive behaviors.

Counselor No. 2 takes a different approach.

*EFFECTIVE*

| *Counselor* | *Client* |
|---|---|
| How can I help you? | I'm not sure. |
| Well, maybe we can find out together. What has been bothering you lately? | Well, my drinking. My wife says that I drink too much. |
| Can you tell me how you feel that drinking is affecting your life? | Well, . . . my wife and I argue a lot. She nags me all of the time. And . . . . well . . . . my job, too, I guess. I've been drinking a lot on the weekends and missing work on Monday morning. |
| Can you be more specific both about your drinking and the problems it is causing you? | I drink about as much as other people that I know. I overdo it and get drunk about twice a week. |
| It sounds like you pal around with some heavy-drinking friends. | Oh, I don't know, they drink as much as most people. (*Slightly defensive*) |
| Why don't you tell me more about the problems in your life that are related to alcohol. I am particularly interested in situations that cause you to drink more than you had planned and problems that arise after you drink too much. | Well . . . my wife is a problem . . . . It's her general attitude toward me and my friends. |

| Please be more specific. What does your wife do and say or not do and say that bothers you? | Well . . . she nags me a lot. She says that I let people take advantage of me. |

The interview continues in this manner. At the end of the session, the counselor says:

| Mr. Smith, I think that it was a very important step for you to come here for help today. I know it was very difficult for you. I feel strongly that between the two of us, we can help you with your problems. The next time we can begin to assess your life in more detail to find out exactly what we can do to make your life more enjoyable and to help you with your drinking problem. | Okay . . . fine. You know . . . I'm glad I came here today. |

In this second example, the counselor requested specific information about the client's drinking *but did not make him defensive by unnecessary confrontation.* He also emphasized positive aspects of the client's behavior and provided him with a feeling of hope for the future. Clients who are given positive expectations for improvement usually do show more therapeutic gains than those who are not.

## ASSESSING IMMEDIATE NEEDS

Most alcoholic clients enter treatment as a result of some crisis in their lives. That is, they often are seeking relief from immediate medical, marital, social, or legal problems. Clients are often hesitant to admit to these problems in many alcoholism counseling centers since many counselors focus almost exclusively on the drinking problem *per se.*

The client may say, "I'm an alcoholic. I need help. I want to stop drinking. I finally have realized what alcohol is doing to my life." In reality, he may be saying, "My boss has threatened to fire me because of my drinking. My wife and kids have just left me. I'm confused. Can you help me?" In essence, the client is saying what he expects that the counselor will want to hear, not what he may really feel. If he were truly honest he might say, "I can't find a job, and I need help. I'm not sure if I want to stop drinking." He is afraid to say this because the counselor might say, "I'm sorry, but this is not an employment agency.

Come back when you're ready to deal with your alcohol problem!"

Within a functional analysis approach, the client's immediate problems are of initial concern since they are related, either as causes or effects, to the excessive drinking pattern.

Actually, the immediate needs of the client can be used therapeutically to motivate him. The counselor can enter into a contractual arrangement with the client in which she states, "I will help you find employment (or solve marital problems, etc.) if you agree to begin making some specific changes in your life and in your drinking that I will suggest to you." This type of contractual arrangement not only helps to insure cooperation with counseling but also decreases the likelihood that the client will simply "use" the counselor. The client understands from the initial session that the counselor's efforts to help him are contingent upon his changing his behavior in a positive direction. The following case illustrates such contracting.

Ralph is a 45-year-old unmarried alcoholic who lives with his mother. He has been drinking heavily for about 15 years and has become an expert at manipulating other people to feel sorry for him and to do everything for him. His entrance into counseling is precipitated by two events in his life: (1) his mother is putting demands on him to become more responsible and has recently told him that he must pay for room and board if he expects to keep living with her, and (2) he has not had steady employment for six months and has had no luck in obtaining a job. After discussing the relationship between the client's drinking and his current problems, the counselor proposes the following contractual arrangement:

The counselor agrees to help the client by (1) assisting him to set up a systematic plan for locating potential employment, contacting employers, and scheduling job interviews, (2) teaching him more effective job-interviewing skills, and (3) assisting him in negotiating an agreement with his mother about room and board.

Each of these efforts at assistance will be contingent upon the following from the client: (1) self-recording of all drinking episodes and specific precipitants of each, (2) arrival on time to every scheduled counseling session, (3) agreement to come to the clinic at two to three randomized times during the week for a breath/alcohol test.

To establish these counseling agreements, the counselor must assess the variety of immediate problems that the client might have. These problems are often marital (e.g., spouse has left or threatened to leave), legal (e.g., foreclosure on the client's house, charges of drunken driving), social (e.g., no friends; acquaintance has threatened to physically harm client), or medical (e.g., high blood pressure, gastritis). Counselors can develop a simple checklist of situations in these categories and request that the client fill this out during the first visit. With certain problems, such as medical or legal ones, the counselor would refer the client to qualified specialists. Again, such referrals can be made contingent upon specific goal-directed behavior changes.

## ASSESSING ALCOHOL ABUSE

The counselor must evaluate the client's history of alcohol use and his present drinking patterns. This can be accomplished by one or several of the following methods: (1) drinking inventories, (2) self-monitoring, (3) reports from others, (4) breath tests, and (5) direct observations in a simulated drinking setting.

Dr. Alan Marlatt of the University of Washington has devised one of the most comprehensive drinking inventories in current use. Known as the "Drinking Profile,"[1] this questionnaire provides detailed information regarding the client's current living situation, family status, employment and income, education, and drinking pattern. The profile is based on a functional analysis of the antecedents and consequences of drinking behavior (as described in Chapter 1). Analysis of the client's drinking is very detailed, including questions about the early development of drinking patterns, current drinking habits, factors associated with drinking, periods of abstinence, drinking locations, attitudes, preferences toward various alcoholic beverages, the manner in which drinks are consumed, reasons for drinking, effects of drinking, motivation to change, and treatment outcome expectancies. The questionnaire can be administered in about one hour. To save time, most of the information regarding living arrangements, education, etc., can be completed by the client at home.

One of the most interesting aspects of this survey is the section on the assessment of motivation. The client is asked about past attempts to seek help and actively change her life. In addition, the client is requested to indicate the results she expects from the treatment. Finally, the client is requested to estimate her chances of a successful outcome based on a 10-point scale, with 1 being little or no chance and 10 being an excellent chance. This method of quantifying expectancy is a very helpful tool that can be used for re-evaluation at various points throughout treatment.

To obtain a *continuous* assessment of drinking behavior, the counselor can request that the client record her drinking episodes on a daily basis. Dr. Linda Sobell and Dr. Mark Sobell of Vanderbilt University have developed an "Alcohol Intake Sheet" on which clients monitor and record daily alcohol consumption.[2] Space is provided on this sheet for the date, specific type of drink, percent of alcohol content in the drink, time when the drink was ordered or prepared, number of sips per drink, amount of the total drink consumed, and the environment in which the drinking occurred. A separate entry is required for each day.

In terms of a functional behavioral analysis, the recording form illustrated in Table 3 is useful. This form provides most of the information that is contained in the "Alcohol Intake Sheet" with the addition of antecedents, consequences, and emotional-cognitive factors associated with drinking. It also is helpful to have clients record situations in which they are tempted to drink but able to resist. This information enables the counselor to assess activities or situations which might be incompatible with drinking and thus serve to decrease its frequency.

As a reliability check on the client's accuracy in reporting drinking behavior, the counselor can enlist the aid of relatives and friends. These individuals can be given recording forms and requested to write down every episode in which they observe the client drinking. However, this method should be employed only with the knowledge and consent of the client.

Another, more objective, method of assessing drinking behavior is by means of breath tests. Various breath tests are available commercially. They range from simple screening devices to more sophisticated models which provide precise blood/alcohol levels via gas chromatography. Clients can self-administer these tests at home, in the presence of a friend or relative. The counselor can telephone the client at random intervals throughout the week, instructing her to self-administer the test. Results can be relayed to the counselor by the friend or relative in attendance. In some counseling settings, it might be more feasible to request the client come to the treatment facility for these tests or even to schedule home visits for them. The counselor must be careful to randomize the administration of these tests so that the client does not learn when it is safe to drink and when it is not.

The counselor can obtain data on the number of hospitalizations for alcohol-related problems or number of arrests for driving under the influence (DUI), driving while intoxicated (DWI), or public drunkenness.

There also are a number of drinking measures to use in direct observation and assessment of alcohol consumption in the treatment setting. With these measures, alcohol is provided to the client and his drinking behavior is observed and recorded either directly or by videotaping. Although these measures have proved invaluable for clinical

TABLE 3. ALCOHOL SELF-MONITORING FORM

| Date | Number and Type of Drinks Consumed | Time of Day | Place and Situation | Antecedent Event | Consequent Event | Mood or Thoughts |
|---|---|---|---|---|---|---|
| 5-10-76 | 3 bourbons with water (1½ ounces each) | 2 p.m. | At home watching TV, alone | Watching television | Left house to buy a bottle for tomorrow | Bored |
| 5-11-76 | 8 bourbons (2 ounces each) | 10 a.m. | In bedroom, alone | Waking up | Passed out | Feeling there is no hope for me |
| 5-12-76 | None | | | | | |
| 5-13-76 | None | | | | | |
| 5-14-76 | 5 beers | 11 p.m. | At home in living room, alone | Getting ready to go to bed— unable to sleep | Fell asleep | Restless, anxious |

research on alcoholism, they may not be feasible or even necessary in most counseling situations. A comprehensive review of these assessment methods is presented by the first author in another publication.[3]

## ASSESSING SOCIAL AND MARITAL BEHAVIORS

### Using Self-Monitoring And Questionnaires

The client's reports of her interpersonal interactions can be obtained either by self-monitoring, standardized questionnaires, or both. Self-monitored data are accumulated by requesting clients to record daily social behaviors in a "behavioral diary." This consists of a small notebook that the client keeps in an accessible location and in which she records number and types of social interactions, duration of the interaction, interpersonal problems, and responses to interpersonal problems. This diary format provides a flexible system by which (depending on the client and the stage of treatment) the client can monitor any number of specific social behaviors (e.g., number of *positive* versus *negative* interactions). The counselor must be careful not to overload the client so that self-monitoring becomes a chore. The counselor might attempt to monitor his own social interactions to determine the feasibility of this approach with a particular client. Usually clients will be able to efficiently monitor two to three behaviors at a time (providing they are not occurring simultaneously).

Checks on the client's accuracy and reliability can be obtained by requesting friends and relatives to record the type and nature of the client's interactions which they observe. These "checks" can be arranged periodically so that a friend might be recording data for only one or two days a week. Additionally, observations of the client's social and leisure-time activities can be assessed weekly or monthly by a relative and/or friend by using a measurement scale such as the Katz Adjustment Scale.[4]

A number of questionnaires which assess a client's general social assertiveness are available. As noted in Chapter 1, this ability to express personal thoughts, feelings, and opinions directly and appropriately is often lacking in alcoholics. Two scales that are easily administered and scored are the *Rathus Assertiveness Schedule*[5] and Dr. Eileen Gambrill's *Assertion Inventory*.[6] The Rathus is a 30-item survey in which clients rate statements (e.g., "I find it embarrassing to return merchandise") on a scale from +3 ("very characteristic of me, extremely descriptive") to -3 ("very uncharacteristic of me, extremely nondescriptive"). The total score is obtained simply by adding the numerical responses (with exceptions noted in the directions).

Gambrill's Assertion Inventory is presented in Table 4. This is a 40-item, self-report survey which provides three types of information about the client's responses to such situations as complimenting a friend, resisting sales pressure, telling another person that she has done something unfair to him, or asking a person who is annoying him in a public situation to change that behavior. The scale provides information on (1) the client's degree of discomfort in each situation, (2) his probability of engaging in that behavior, and (3) situations that the client wishes to handle more assertively.

With either of these assertiveness measures, it would be advisable to establish norms on the alcoholic population being served. This could be accomplished simply by administering either test to all clients until an adequate sample of 25 to 50 clients is completed. Knowledge about the average (mean) score and the range of scores for the population will enable the counselor to compare each new client's assertiveness score to determine his level of assertiveness in relation to his peers.

Since marital problems also are characteristic of alcoholic clients, marital assessment is often necessary. Dr. Nathan Azrin of Anna State Hospital in Illinois has devised a Marital Happiness Scale[7] that is depicted in Table 5.

This scale contains 10 separate marital areas: household responsibilities, child rearing, social activities, money, communication, sex, occupational or academic progress, personal independence, and general happiness. The client simply rates herself on each of these dimensions on a 10-point scale (1 = completely unhappy; 10 = completely happy). This scale can assist the counselor and client to pinpoint specific marital concerns that may be associated with problem drinking.

## The Counselor's Observations

An important adjunct to all these self-report measures is direct behavioral observations. Behavioral assessments enable the counselor to evaluate the accuracy and reliability of the client's reports about himself and allow for a more detailed analysis of subtle aspects of the client's interpersonal response style. Interpersonal interactions are assessed by observing the client role play several simulated social encounters. Another counselor, a secretary, or a volunteer worker could play the part of the interpersonal partner in these scenes, with the client's counselor observing and taking notes. Videotaping these interactions can be very helpful in later evaluating the client's behavior in more detail.

The role-played scenes might include several different social situa-

## TABLE 4. THE ASSERTION INVENTORY*

Many people experience difficulty in handling interpersonal situations requiring them to assert themselves in some way, for example, turning down a request, asking a favor, giving someone a compliment, expressing disapproval or approval, etc. Please indicate your degree of discomfort or anxiety in the space provided before each situation listed below. Utilize the following scale to indicate degree of discomfort:

1 = none
2 = a little
3 = a fair amount
4 = much
5 = very much

Then, go over the list a second time and indicate after each item the probability or likelihood of your displaying the behavior if actually presented with the situation.† For example, if you rarely apologize when you are at fault, you would mark a "4" after that item. Utilize the following scale to indicate response probability:

1 = always do it
2 = usually do it
3 = do it about half the time
4 = rarely do it
5 = never do it

†NOTE. It is important to cover your discomfort ratings (located in front of the items) while indicating response probability. Otherwise, one rating may contaminate the other and a realistic assessment of your behavior is unlikely. To correct for this, place a piece of paper over your discomfort ratings while responding to the situations a second time for response probability.

| Degree of Discomfort | | Situation | Response Probability |
|---|---|---|---|
| _____ | 1. | Turn down a request to borrow your car | _____ |
| _____ | 2. | Compliment a friend | _____ |
| _____ | 3. | Ask a favor of someone | _____ |
| _____ | 4. | Resist sales pressure | _____ |
| _____ | 5. | Apologize when you are at fault | _____ |
| | 6. | Turn down a request for a meeting or date | |
| _____ | | | _____ |
| _____ | 7. | Admit fear and request consideration | _____ |

27

*Table 4, cont.*

| Degree of Discomfort | | Situation | Response Probability |
|---|---|---|---|
| | 8. | Tell a person you are intimately in-volved with when he/she says or does something that bothers you | |
| _____ | 9. | Ask for a raise | _____ |
| _____ | 10. | Admit ignorance in some area | _____ |
| _____ | 11. | Turn down a request to borrow money | _____ |
| _____ | 12. | Ask personal questions | _____ |
| _____ | 13. | Turn off a talkative friend | _____ |
| _____ | 14. | Ask for constructive criticism | _____ |
| _____ | 15. | Initiate a conversation with a stranger | _____ |
| _____ | 16. | Compliment a person you are roman-tically involved with or interested in | _____ |
| _____ | 17. | Request a meeting or a date with a person | _____ |
| _____ | 18. | Your initial request for a meeting is turned down and you ask the person again at a later time | _____ |
| _____ | 19. | Admit confusion about a point under discussion and ask for clarification | _____ |
| _____ | 20. | Apply for a job | _____ |
| _____ | 21. | Ask whether you have offended someone | _____ |
| _____ | 22. | Tell someone that you like them | _____ |
| _____ | 23. | Request expected service when such is not forthcoming, e.g., in a restaurant | _____ |
| _____ | 24. | Discuss openly with the person his/her criticism of your behavior | _____ |
| _____ | 25. | Return defective items, e.g., store or restaurant | _____ |
| _____ | 26. | Express an opinion that differs from that of the person you are talking to | _____ |
| _____ | 27. | Resist sexual overtures when you are not interested | _____ |
| _____ | 28. | Tell the person when you feel he/she has done something that is unfair to you | _____ |
| _____ | 29. | Accept a date | _____ |

*Table 4, cont.*

| Degree of Discomfort | | Situation | Response Probability |
|---|---|---|---|
| | 30. | Tell someone good news about your-self | |
| _____ | 31. | Resist pressure to drink | _____ |
| | 32. | Resist a significant person's unfair demand | |
| _____ | | | _____ |
| _____ | 33. | Quit a job | _____ |
| _____ | 34. | Resist pressure to "turn on" | _____ |
| | 35. | Discuss openly with the person his/her criticism of your work | |
| _____ | | | _____ |
| _____ | 36. | Request the return of borrowed items | _____ |
| _____ | 37. | Receive compliments | _____ |
| | 38. | Continue to converse with someone who disagrees with you | |
| _____ | | | _____ |
| | 39. | Tell a friend or someone with whom you work when he/she says or does something that bothers you | |
| _____ | | | _____ |
| | 40. | Ask a person who is annoying you in a public situation to stop | |
| _____ | | | _____ |

Lastly, please indicate the situations you would like to handle more assertively by placing a circle around the item number.

*Reprinted with permission from E. D. Gambrill and C. A. Richey. An assertion inventory for use in assessment and research. *Behavior Therapy*, 1975, *6*, 550-561.

tions requiring effective interpersonal skills. Each scene is written on an index card in the following manner.

*Scene 1* (Initiation of social interaction)
    You are at a large social gathering and you know only one or two of the guests. A number of people are standing around in small groups conversing with one another. You walk over to a group of four or five people. Two of the people in the group turn to look at you. You say:

## TABLE 5. MARITAL HAPPINESS SCALE*

This scale is intended to estimate your *current* happiness with your marriage in each of the ten areas listed. You are to circle one of the numbers (1-10) beside each marriage area. Numbers toward the left end of the ten-unit scale indicate some degree of unhappiness and numbers toward the right end of the scale reflect varying degrees of happiness. Ask yourself this question as you rate each marriage area: "If my partner continues to act in the future as he (she) is acting *today* with respect to this marriage area, how happy will I be *with this area of our marriage*?" In other words, state according to the numerical scale (1-10) exactly how you feel today. Try to exclude all feelings of yesterday and concentrate only on the feelings of today in each of the marital areas. Also try not to allow one category to influence the results of theother categories.

| | Completely Unhappy | | | | | | Completely Happy | | | |
|---|---|---|---|---|---|---|---|---|---|---|
| Household responsibilities | 1 | 2 | 3 | 4 | 5 | 6 | 7 | 8 | 9 | 10 |
| Rearing of children | 1 | 2 | 3 | 4 | 5 | 6 | 7 | 8 | 9 | 10 |
| Social activities | 1 | 2 | 3 | 4 | 5 | 6 | 7 | 8 | 9 | 10 |
| Money | 1 | 2 | 3 | 4 | 5 | 6 | 7 | 8 | 9 | 10 |
| Communication | 1 | 2 | 3 | 4 | 5 | 6 | 7 | 8 | 9 | 10 |
| Sex | 1 | 2 | 3 | 4 | 5 | 6 | 7 | 8 | 9 | 10 |
| Occupational or academic progress | 1 | 2 | 3 | 4 | 5 | 6 | 7 | 8 | 9 | 10 |
| Personal independence | 1 | 2 | 3 | 4 | 5 | 6 | 7 | 8 | 9 | 10 |
| Spouse independence | 1 | 2 | 3 | 4 | 5 | 6 | 7 | 8 | 9 | 10 |
| General happiness | 1 | 2 | 3 | 4 | 5 | 6 | 7 | 8 | 9 | 10 |

Name _____

Date _____

*Reprinted with permission from N. H. Azrin, B. J. Naster, and R. Jones. Reciprocity counseling: A rapid learning-based procedure for marital counseling. *Behaviour Research and Therapy,* 1973, *11,* 365-382.

*Scene 2* (Alcoholic beverage refusal)

You are driving home from work with some of your friends. One of them says, "Hey, let's stop at that bar up ahead and get a few beers." You say:_____

*Scene 3* (Expression of negative feelings)

You have spent all day working on a special project for your spouse. You have worked very carefully and have given up your favorite weekend recreational activity to please your spouse with this project. He comes over to you and says, "What a sloppy job! I knew that I should have done that myself!" You say: _____
_____ .

*The client's verbal and nonverbal reactions to these scenes can be rated along several dimensions. These include the following:*

*Nonverbal Dimensions*

1. *Eye contact:* The total amount of time the client looked directly at the other individual during a specified period of response time.
2. *Gestures:* The presence or absence of hand and arm gestures appropriate to the response.
3. *Posture:* A rating of 1 to 5 with 1 indicating a stiff posture and 5 indicating a relaxed posture.
4. *Affect:* A rating of 1 to 5 with 1 indicating little or no emotional expression and 5 indicating appropriate emotional expressions.
5. *Smiles:* Total number of smiles during a specified period of response time.

*Verbal Dimensions*

1. *Loudness:* A rating of 1 to 5 with 1 indicating a soft, inaudible voice and 5 indicating an appropriate sound intensity.
2. *Questions:* Total number of questions asked.
3. *Compliance:* Presence or absence of, or total number of, statements in which the client complies with an unreasonable request.
4. *Positive comments:* Total number of positive comments.
5. *Negative comments:* Total number of negative comments.
6. *Requests for new behavior:* Presence or absence of a request for the other individual to change her behavior.
7. *Self-reference statements:* Total number of statements referring to the client.
8. *Other-directed statements:* Total number of questions or comments which refer to the other individual.

Certainly not all these components can be rated accurately without the aid of videotape or numerous raters. In most cases, the counselor would observe two or three role-played scenes with the client, and on the basis of these global observations, she would decide which interpersonal elements to rate. Also, the components chosen would be a function of the type of scene being role played.

Another method of assessing social interaction is through unstructured interpersonal encounters. With this method, the client is simply requested to converse with another individual (e.g., spouse) for 20 to 30 minutes. The counselor observes the interaction from an inconspicuous location (ideally from behind a one-way mirror). Of course, in every case, the client is aware that she is being observed and has given her full informed consent for the behavioral assessment.

In the remaining chapters, we shall consider more details regarding behavioral assessment as they relate to specific behavior patterns (e.g., marital interactions).

## ASSESSING SOCIAL-PSYCHOLOGICAL FUNCTIONING

### Emotional States

Assessment of the client's mood or feelings is necessary since many alcoholics complain of anxiety, depression, or restlessness either prior to or after a drinking episode. These emotional states usually are assessed by means of self-reports and mood inventories. As with social behaviors, the client can be requested to keep a diary of his daily mood states, particularly as they precipitate drinking. The client might rate specific moods each day on a 10-point scale as follows (Figure 2). It also is important for the client to rate positive emotional states, such as feelings of accomplishment or personal happiness. Alcoholic clients seldom are as aware of their positive moods as they are of their negative ones. The counselor must determine, on the basis of this self-assessment by the client, the relationship between specific mood states and periods of both drinking and sobriety.

In addition to reporting on moods *per se,* the client should be encouraged to pinpoint specific social, cognitive, or environmental stimuli associated with positive and negative mood states. Behavioral counseling is geared toward remediation of the client's responses to these situations or his efforts to change them. These *behavioral* changes, in turn, lead to improvements in emotionl feelings.

Specific inventories, such as the Fear Survey Schedule[8] and the Reinforcement Survey Schedule,[9] are useful in emotional assessment. On the Fear Survey Schedule the client rates anxiety or fear in relation to objects, situations, or persons listed. The Reinforcement Survey

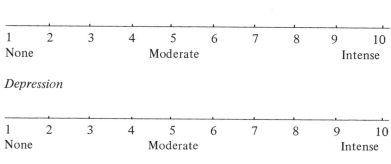

FIGURE 2.    EXAMPLE OF POSSIBLE MOOD RATING SCALE

*Anxiety*

| 1    | 2 | 3 | 4 | 5        | 6 | 7 | 8 | 9 | 10      |
|------|---|---|---|----------|---|---|---|---|---------|
| None |   |   |   | Moderate |   |   |   |   | Intense |

*Depression*

| 1    | 2 | 3 | 4 | 5        | 6 | 7 | 8 | 9 | 10      |
|------|---|---|---|----------|---|---|---|---|---------|
| None |   |   |   | Moderate |   |   |   |   | Intense |

Schedule also lists a wide variety of activities (e.g., playing tennis) and situations (e.g., being complimented or being with a loved one). On this inventory, the client simply rates positive feelings that accrue from experiencing each situation listed. This assessment tool often provides a list of situations that are incompatible with excessive drinking (e.g., going shopping with a loved one).

The Beck Depression Inventory[10] provides an excellent analysis of depression. The analysis of depression is particularly important with female alcoholics since they are more likely than male alcoholics to demonstrate serious clinical depression that may require intensive intervention or short-term hospitalization. The Beck Inventory consists of a number of items related to sleeping difficulties, listlessness, suicidal thoughts, outlook for the future, failure, and feelings, such as boredom, guilt, self-disappointment, and sadness. The client simply circles one statement that best applies to her in each of 21 series of statements. For example, she might choose, "I feel that I would be better off dead."

*Verification of mood data.* Determining validity is one of the major difficulties in assessing data on moods. That is, does the client actually experience anxiety when he reports it to the counselor? Unfortunately, the counselor cannot experience what the client is feeling and, thus, must rely on his verbal reports. To deal with this problem, the counselor must use as many other sources of information as possible. It is helpful to develop behavioral definitions for emotions so that their occurrence can be observed by friends, relatives, or the counselor. For example, **anxiety** could be defined in terms of trembling, flushing of the face, inappropriate smiling or laughter, cracking voice, etc. When the client is in situations in which he reports anxiety, significant others can be requested to record the appearance of any of these anxiety *behaviors.* **Depression** can be defined behaviorally in terms of decreased motor activity, sleep disturbance, crying, flat or depressed social expression, or decreased sexual activity. Both the counselor and friends and relatives in the home environment can record instances or frequency of these behaviors, particularly as they relate to specific social-environmental situations and drinking episodes.

## ASSESSING VOCATIONAL AND RECREATIONAL BEHAVIORS

Assessing the client's occupational status and her range of recreational activities is important in alcoholism treatment. Often, alcoholic clients are unemployed or holding positions which are not satisfying to them. Since stable work patterns are incompatible with chronic heavy drinking, monitoring these patterns is helpful. Clients can record and report the number of days late for work, number of days left work early, and number of days of sick leave or leave without pay. It is possible to check the accuracy of these reports through periodic contacts with employers. Such contact would also provide an index of work performance. An easier method of checking reports is requesting clients to supply their weekly or monthly paycheck stubs.

The counselor also may wish to assess behaviors necessary to obtain employment. For example, does the client know how to fill out a job application with particular reference to difficult questions (e.g., If you have been unemployed in the last six months, please give specific reasons)? Does the client have the necessary interpersonal skills to sell himself in a job interview? The counselor can assess these behaviors by setting up a simulated role-playing situation requiring the client to apply for employment.

Recreational activities can be evaluated easily by requesting the client and a relative or friend to record all leisure-time activities each week. The type of event, its relative positive value to the client, and the length of time involved should be recorded. Dr. Peter Lewinsohn and his colleagues have developed a Pleasant Events Schedule which assesses various types of leisure-time activities.[11]

## Footnotes

1. G. A. Marlatt. The drinking profile: A questionnaire for the behavioral assessment of alcoholism. In E. J. Mash and L. G. Terdal, eds., *Behavior therapy assessment: Diagnosis and evaluation.* New York: Springer, 1977.

2. L. C. Sobell and M. B. Sobell. A self-feedback technique to monitor drinking behavior in alcoholics. *Behaviour Research and Therapy,* 1973, *11,* 237-238.

3. P. M. Miller. Assessment of addictive behaviors. In A. R. Ciminero, K. S. Calhoun, and H. E. Adams, eds., *Handbook of behavioral assessment.* New York: John Wiley and Sons, 1977.

4. M. M. Katz and S. B. Lyerly. Methods for measuring adjustment behavior in the community: 1. Rationale, description, discriminatory validity, and scale development. *Psychological Reports,* 1963, *13,* 503-535.

5. S. A. Rathus. A 30-item schedule for assessing assertive behavior. *Behavior Therapy,* 1973, *4,* 398-406.

6. E. D. Gambrill and C. A. Richey. An assertion inventory for use in assessment and research. *Behavior Therapy,* 1975, *6,* 550-561.

7. N. H. Azrin, B. J. Naster, and R. Jones. Reciprocity counseling: A rapid learning-based procedure for marital counseling. *Behaviour Research and Therapy,* 1973, *11,* 365-382.

8. J. Wolpe. *The practice of behavior therapy.* New York: Pergamon Press, Inc., 1973.

9. J. R. Cautela and R. Kastenbaum. A reinforcement survey schedule for use in therapy, training, and research. *Psychological Reports,* 1967, *20,* 1115-1130.

10. A. T. Beck, C. H. Ward, M. Mendelson, J. Mock, and J. Erbaugh. An inventory for measuring depression. *Archives of General Psychiatry,* 1961, *4,* 561-571.

11. P. M. Lewinsohn and J. Libet. Pleasant events, activity schedules, and depression. *Journal of Abnormal Psychology,* 1972, *79,* 291-295.

# 3 Establishing a Treatment Plan

Often, a counselor gathers a wealth of information about a client but uses little of it in developing the treatment plan. This happens when the counselor fails to systematize the information into a meaningful whole. Using a behavioral approach helps to avoid this error. A major contribution of behaviorism is the emphasis on developing a treatment plan based on interpretation of the assessment material. The assessment data are divided into three major behavioral areas: excesses, deficits, and assets. This approach gives the counselor and client a structure in which to function. Expectations become clear. Misunderstandings are less likely to arise and, if they do occur, are resolved more easily. With the behavioral approach, progress can be evaluated not only at the end of treatment but also at any point in counseling.

In this chapter, we will discuss ways of describing and listing the client's strengths and weaknesses so that therapeutic goals are more evenly set and less assessment data are lost.

## IDENTIFYING BEHAVIORAL EXCESSES

**Behavioral excesses** are behaviors which have become problematic because (1) they are used too frequently (e.g., crying), (2) have generalized to other situations (e.g., when one is angry at everyone because her job is not going well), (3) are too intense (e.g., a loud, harsh tone of voice), or (4) are used to the exclusion of other behaviors, which causes additional problems (e.g., the client who is usually aggressive in dealing with his partner blocks communication).

The most obvious behavioral excess of the problem drinker is her use of alcohol. However, this same obviousness may cloud the assessment so that the counselor fails to attend to the associated excesses. For example, the individual who drinks too much also may be excessively depressed, passive, dependent on others to fulfill material needs.

Working to restrict or eliminate alcohol consumption may not automatically eliminate the associated excesses. The counselor must be aware of them to anticipate their impact and include them in treatment.

Mr. A. is a client having excesses associated with alcohol. Treatment to restrict alcohol consumption had proved effective, but unforeseen complications arose. Certain excesses that had been masked by the alcohol consumption became evident. The excesses of most immediate concern were Mr. A.'s dependency, especially on perceived authority figures (such as his counselor), and his passivity in relating to most people.

A program was devised to handle these "new" life problems. Since dependency and passivity are intimately related, they were treated together by assertion training. An excerpt from the program is described below. Mr. A. is in a restaurant with several friends who drink heavily. Although it is known that Mr. A. no longer drinks alcoholic beverages, one person persists in encouraging him to drink. The problem is presented in an assertion training group, and group members assume the parts of Mr. A.'s friends.

*Mr. M.:* How about a cocktail, A., you look like you need a pick-me-up.

*Mr. A.:* No, M. I'm not drinking tonight.

*Mr. M.:* Oh, what a drag, you're putting a damper on the party.

*Mr. J.:* (*In a sympathetic tone*) Leave him alone, M. He said he wasn't drinking.

*Ms. T.:* J. is right. I think it's terrible that you're pressuring A. Why don't you just stop!

(Mr. J. has jumped to A.'s defense, allowing A. to become dependent on J. to solve the problem.)

The counselor stops the scene and gets reactions from the group.

*Mr. A.:* I just can't handle it.

*Mr. M.:* I think he wants me to talk him into getting a drink.

*Mr. J.:* I know just how he feels.

*Ms. T.:* I'm a little angry that A. couldn't be firmer with M. Why did we have to get into it?

*Counselor:* Any suggestions on how A. could have handled the problem himself?

The participants offer alternative solutions; some role play a more appropriate A. Mr. A. tries out some new responses, picks one most comfortable for him, and practices it.

## IDENTIFYING BEHAVIORAL DEFICITS

It is often said that the alcoholic masks her shortcomings by drinking heavily. Clinical evaluation indicates there is much truth to this. The alcoholic client often can more easily identify behavioral deficits than behavioral excesses. In fact, clients will most probably consider their deficits as primary causes of alcohol abuse, if they consider behavioral reasons at all. As with excesses, deficits may be grouped into categories, such as overt, covert, social, and physiological.

A client has a **behavioral deficit** if he completely lacks a particular desired behavior or fails to exhibit it (a) frequently enough, (b) intensely enough, or (c) at the appropriate time and place. The typical alcoholic client has a number of deficits which have been masked by the excessive alcohol consumption. Unless these deficits are corrected, the client may not be able to replace alcohol consumption with other behaviors, so returning to alcohol abuse is probable.

The client may have had a certain behavior in his repertoire, but as alcohol consumption increased, the desired behavior was reduced or eliminated. Examples of such behaviors are personal maintenance tasks, cooking, attending social functions, and completing work duties. These behaviors enhance the quality of life and indicate a person's positive self-concept. As alcoholism consumes more of a person's time and energy, each area of his life suffers.

Some counselors feel that an alcoholic's work is the last area to break down. Joan B. was a client whose deficits hindered her from obtaining employment. She did not qualify for positions she had held earlier in her life, and she was unable to complete successful interviews for any job. Her appearance was unkempt, and she had no plan for explaining time lapse in employment. Time was spent on these deficits to prepare her for job interviews. The interrelatedness of these areas (appearance, interview behavior, salable job skills) was discussed with Ms. B., and a plan to rebuild her marketability was designed (see Chapter 9).

## IDENTIFYING BEHAVIORAL ASSETS

**Behavioral assets** are skills and talents, positive social behaviors, past experiences and accomplishments, desire for future strivings, and any other positive behaviors which the client possesses. Assets may not be apparent at first glance. However, even those that are comparatively minor will be useful in treatment in the following ways: (1) they will be enhanced and developed and (2) they will be used as a basis for improvement in areas of deficits and elimination of excesses.

The broader and more complete the evaluation of assets, the more freedom there is in developing the treatment plan.

A list of assets compiled by the counselor and a client, Joe T., follows.

1. *Interpersonal:* Mr. T. is a good conversationalist, has an attractive appearance, and has a sense of humor.
2. *Motivational:* Mr. T. desires to re-enter employment and to save his marriage.
3. *Sexual:* Although he and his wife did not have a satisfactory sexual relationship at present, they had had in years previous to the alcohol problem. Mr. T. was offered affection from his wife and was able to accept it.
4. *Hobbies:* At one time the client belonged to a chess club and a Saturday morning softball team. He also spent time reading historical books.
5. *Self-Concept:* Although Mr. T. feels he is a disappointment to himself and his family, he does remember when he was an effective adult and wonders if he could still have some of that effectiveness in him.

As counseling progresses, the list will expand. The counselor should use assets whenever possible. In the case of Mr. T., the interpersonal assets were used in group sessions: he was reinforced for his sense of humor whenever he used it to tone down self-criticism. The fine line between humor and sarcasm was noted, however, and steps were taken to hinder the generalization of sarcasm.

## DEVELOPING GOALS

### Factors Influencing Goals
As earlier mentioned, when the client is actively involved in goal development, commitment to its attainment is more likely. Involving the client in goal setting also is consistent with a general therapeutic goal of behavior modification: teaching skills that can be added to the client's existing repertoire of problem-solving skills. In this approach, the client is the change agent with the counselor acting as guide and consultant.

In goal setting, the client's *expectations* will become apparent and misconceptions may be changed. The counselor should realize the importance of the *therapeutic relationship* in this and all stages of client-helper interaction.

As with other modes of therapy, behavior modification is more effective when the client is able to trust the counselor enough to disclose problems and make a commitment to change. Counselors have their own styles of relating, and they will develop the assets of themselves and clients with experience. They should be aware of the clients' reactions to them. The use of certain words, tone of voice, style of dress, their sex, or race may affect the therapeutic relationship. Audio or videotapes of counseling sessions may assist counselors in determining their counseling assets.

Setting long- and short-term goals is dependent on (1) the extent and seriousness of the client's problems, (2) his motivation, (3) the setting, (4) projected treatment time, (5) preference of the client and counselor, and (6) cooperation of significant others.

*Seriousness of condition* sometimes dictates priorities. For example, if the client must immediately discontinue drinking or risk death through physical complications, the seriousness of the condition establishes this immediate withdrawal as first treatment priority. Another example would be the client who is so severely depressed that his perceptions of self and of the world around are distorted.

The *client's motivation* also will affect goal setting. The counselor may perceive that the client doubts change can occur or is willing to expend little energy on it. In that case, the counselor would suggest a first treatment goal that would show significant results quickly. This initial success would help motivate the client.

Building motivation through a series of successes can be done even with difficult problems. A complex problem can be divided into manageable components which are more accessible to quick change. An example of such strategy is the case of Jim, a young man who wished to enter trade school in auto mechanics. Unemployed for over a year, he felt overwhelmed by the admission procedure. The counselor suggested the process could be divided into several discrete steps and thus made more manageable.

Using the following checklist, Jim was able to complete the procedure and gain admission.

1. Call admissions office for forms.
2. Fill out personal history section.
3. Call high school to forward transcript.

4. Request letter of recommendation from
   a. two high school teachers
   b. former employer
   c. counselor
5. Complete application, sign, and mail.
6. Request personal interview.

Success in each step was reinforced by the counselor with praise and verbal recognition and by Jim who gave himself tickets to the professional baseball game each time he accomplished a task.

The *setting, significant others,* and *projected time in treatment* may act as natural limitations to goal setting. Certain goals would require an inpatient setting or complete environmental change. If this is impossible for counselor and client, modification of the goal is necessary. The presence or absence of significant others also may help set priorities. For example, if the client wishes to become sexually active with another but does not presently have a partner, other short-term goals, such as meeting and forming relationships, will supercede the goal of sexual contact. The projected treatment time, whether weeks or months, also will limit goal setting. The public often has the impression that behavioral techniques will affect change in four or five sessions. When the problems are multiple, complex, or of long duration (which is usual with alcoholism), treatment is prolonged.

## Pinpointing Client's Problems

First, the counselor and client use the lists of behavioral excesses, deficits, and assets to *pinpoint the client's problems.* These problems become the basis for goal setting. Before this pinpointing, the client's complaint was, "Everyone walks all over me." After exploration with the counselor, it is defined as my spouse and boss (everyone), but not my children or co-workers, neglect to consider my opinion when making decisions that will affect me (walk all over me). The counselor and client were able to *specify the problems* by discussing the situation and by gathering data. In this way the client and counselor use the behavioral list to identify and describe the client's problems.

## Grouping And Ranking Problems

The client and counselor should examine each category of the behavioral list, specifying problems in the manner just mentioned. Related problems should be listed together, and a determination of how they are related should be made. Here the seriousness and bothersomeness of certain problems make them treatment priorities.

Next, the problems are placed into two *goal categories,* long-range and short-range. This determination is made by (a) need for resolution, (b) preferences of client and counselor, (c) place the problem holds in the chain of related problems, and (d) ease with which change may be affected. A long-range goal may be relocation of the client to a more pleasant neighborhood. This may be dependent, however, on the shorter-range goal of attaining employment that will make the move economically feasible. Or, a couple may wish a more satisfactory sexual relationship, but their general communication must first be adjusted.

After the problems are grouped into these two categories, they must be ranked within the categories. Especially at the beginning of treatment, it is often frustrating and counterproductive to have the client measuring and using therapeutic techniques on more than two or three problems at a time. Therefore, within each category of long- and short-term goals, priorities must be set.

## NEGOTIATING

After possible goals have been developed by the methods just described, the counselor and client must negotiate the decision on them. Many clients are shocked that they are not only invited, but expected, to decide on goals. They come into treatment expecting the counselor to decide when, what, where, and how changes should be made. The counselor needs to help the client realize his participation is necessary because he (the client) is responsible for his behavior and any decisions to change it. That is, *the client is the designated change agent.* The counselor should always consider herself a consultant. The temptation for the counselor to be decision-maker is always great, especially since the more global picture is often evident. Yet, part of treatment itself is the client's acceptance of goal-setting responsibility.

It is necessary to understand why the client wishes to set particular goals. Thus, probing and guiding are a part of the counselor's work. This counseling period may be the first time in a while that the client has been requested to make decisions that will have far-reaching effects on him, and often on others. Therefore, the counselor may need to *shape* the client's decision-making behavior. Steps in problem-solving (see Chapters 5, 6, 7, 8, 9) will assist the client. Listing consequences (both positive and negative) of change in a particular area and alternatives to the solution of the problem will assist the novice negotiator. It is often helpful to have the client verbalize his thoughts while deciding on goals. In this way, faulty thinking may be corrected and appropriate reinforcement given by the counselor.

At times the counselor may have to elicit questions remaining unverbalized by the client. This is a good way to show that she can *empathize* with the client. As the client progresses in his involvement as negotiator, there will be many opportunities for the counselor to verbally and nonverbally reinforce him.

The counselor may find it necessary to re-direct the client's attention to certain problems that may have been ignored or overlooked. If a client is not ready to look at a problem very closely, it should be placed on the list of long-range goals.

The client is actively involved in two other aspects of goals negotiation: setting of the pace for change and treatment technique used. When the client determines how much can be accomplished between sessions and how much time is needed to attain a particular goal, the probability of meeting these time limits increases.

Of course, it is the counselor who is knowledgeable about the available treatment techniques to correct a particular problem. However, when a selection among appropriate techniques or adjustment within the chosen technique can be made jointly, the client is more committed to its use. Treatment choice also will be limited by such considerations as time consumed (e.g., relaxation training will take about 20 minutes, twice a day), aesthetics (e.g., using the punishing image of the client vomiting may be unacceptable to the client or the counselor), and health (e.g., chemical aversion is contraindicated when the client suffers certain physical problems). Generally, the counselor will present a description of treatment alternatives and discuss each with the client before they decide which is most appropriate.

Below is an excerpt from a session in which the client and counselor decide how to treat Mary L.'s excessive thoughts on drinking after six weeks of abstinence. She and the counselor discuss her disturbing thoughts, and the counselor presents a program designed to contain the problem:

| Counselor | Client |
|---|---|
| There are a few different ways of handling the disturbing thoughts. One is to use *STOP Therapy* each time the thought occurs. (The counselor then presents a rationale and demonstrates the procedure, first having the client verbalize the thought and loudly say | But they're too easy. I can't see how they'd work. |

"Stop!" and then having her practice the procedure nonverbally.) The other is to use the Premack Principle. (Again she describes and demonstrates the procedure. These are presented in detail in Chapter 8.)

They certainly are simple to use. These techniques have been used on many people with problems similar to yours. They have even been shown to work experimentally. (The counselor gives several examples of problems treated by the two methods and suggests both can be used concurrently).

Well, let's try the second one, the Premack Principle.

Fine, why don't we set it up for the next two weeks and then evaluate the progress we've made with this technique.

## WRITING CONTRACTUAL TREATMENT AGREEMENTS

Negotiations will lead to verbal and written contractual agreements between the client and the counselor. Although verbal agreements are appropriate for session-to-session assignments, generally it is best to design a written contract after goals have been agreed upon. The contract should include a statement of problems and long- and short-term goals for each, time limits, treatments to be used, responsibilities of the client and the counselor, methods for evaluating change, and termination date. The contract may be as formal or informal as desired, as long as both persons understand the terms. A detailed description of the procedure for setting up contracts is given in Chapter 6.

The contract is merely a summary of the steps which went before it: the analysis of assessment data to determine the client's behavioral excesses, deficits, and assets; the determination of problem areas; and formulations of long- and short-term goals and procedures needed to accomplish them (see Form I).

Setting *goal priorities* helps keep counseling sessions on target. Without priorities, it is easy to work piece-meal on many problems during a session and therefore accomplish very little. Working in

*FORM 1. CLIENT-COUNSELOR CONTRACT AGREEMENT*

The following agreement is based on information obtained during initial data-gathering sessions between the client _____ and the counselor _____ . We have agreed to the following.

A. Problem-list

1. Short-Term Goals     Treatment To Be Used     Time Limit
   (listed in priority)

   a.
   b.
   c.
   d.

2. Long-Term Goals     Treatment To Be Used     Time Limit
   (listed in priority)

   a.
   b.
   c.
   d.

B. The client, _____ , has agreed to the following responsibilities (list such items as number of sessions, outside-session tasks, fees, etc.):

   a.
   b.
   c.

The counselor, _____ , has agreed to the following responsibilities (number of sessions, confidentiality, availability in case of emergencies, etc.):

   a.
   b.
   c.

C. Evaluation procedure to determine goal attainment in each area will consist of the following (Describe pre-post evaluation, such as food-alcohol levels, self-monitoring, observation by others, verification by pay stubs, etc.)

D. Termination (Describe contingencies for both positive and negative termination.)

*Form 1, cont.*

E.   Re-negotiation procedure (Describe).

We agree to adhere to this contract unless re-negotiation occurs or until goals are attained. Any break by those involved voids the contract.

Signed

_____          _____
Witness                                                        Client

_____          _____
Date                                                            Counselor

_____          _____

limited areas helps keep the client from becoming overwhelmed and feeling hopeless. It also teaches goal-directed behavior, something that frequently is missing in clients.

Including in the contract *time limitations* for attaining a goal also keeps sessions on target and trains the client in goal-directed behavior.

Additionally, time limitations can be used to determine the client's motivation. If the interim time schedule is kept, indications are good that the client has grasped how to carry out treatment and is, in fact, carrying out assigned tasks between sessions. The inverse also is true; in that case, the counselor should discuss with the client the problems encountered in attaining the interim time goal. Perhaps the client has not fully understood how to carry out the assignment or has not grasped the necessity for carrying out the task in the agreed manner and time. Also, the client might not be committed to the goal set; re-negotiation would be necessary. (In Chapter 10, we discuss methods for monitoring intrasession data.) Tentative re-negotiation and termination dates may be contracted at this time. Although re-negotiation may occur at any point in treatment, prearrangement for it prevents switching treatment techniques too soon if change is not occurring. It also provides a systematic manner for changing goal priorities. As the target behavior change is accomplished, other behaviors are affected and certain goals may be more accessible or even unnecessary as areas of concern. Natural time limits, such as the client's relocation in another city or the resumption of school or employment, may occur. An evaluation of progress every six weeks (the number is arbitrary, but appears long enough to allow change to occur) is appropriate.

Contracts make clear the therapeutic responsibility which the client and the counselor will assume individually and mutually.

Such general **client responsibilities** will include accomplishment of assigned intersession tasks, recording of data, and discussion of material concerning target problems and treatment. Specific responsibilities will include such factors as the number of times treatment techniques are used daily.

General **counselor responsibilities** will include confidentiality, availability or coverage for emergencies, involvement of the client in decision making, and referral of clients with whom the counselor cannot work. Specific responsibilities include the development of a treatment plan suited to the individual client. The plan should offer treatment strategies that are the simplest, easiest, and most inexpensive to the client in terms of time, energy, and money.

# 4 Relaxation Training

## IDENTIFYING ANXIETY AND ITS CAUSES

Feelings of anxiety, agitation, and restlessness are frequent precipitants of excessive drinking for many clients. Although anxiety is not considered to be as crucial a factor in the etiology of excessive drinking as was once believed, many problem drinkers report that it is a significant problem. Therapeutic techniques designed to reduce tension appear to be especially useful with younger, less chronic alcoholics. As chronicity of the alcohol problem develops, however, anxiety seems to play less of a role in *initiating* drinking episodes. Recent studies indicate that female alcoholics and high school and college-aged problem drinkers can benefit substantially from relaxation training.

In applying relaxation training, the counselor must realize that anxiety is not a clinical entity in and of itself. Specific social, emotional, and cognitive problems related to anxiety must be considered. Merely teaching anxiety-reduction techniques is never sufficient without enabling the client to deal more effectively with the specific problem situations eliciting anxiety and problem drinking. Techniques for accomplishing this goal are described in subsequent chapters.

As an example, suppose that Tom B. feels very nervous and upset when he interacts with people whom he considers to be his superiors. Tom is a drug salesman and must call on physicians and discuss his products with them. To deal with his anxiety in these situations, Tom has been increasing his drinking both before and after his meetings with customers. Via relaxation training, Tom's counselor helps him to reduce his anxiety. Unfortunately, anxiety reduction will only partially solve Tom's problem. Two important factors related to his anxiety with physicians are (1) his inability to behave assertively and with self-assurance when trying to get his points across to them, and (2) his irrational, self-defeating thought patterns prior to his meetings ("These doctors are highly educated and knowledgeable people. What if they ask me a question that I can't answer? What will they think of me?"). Thus, reducing Tom's anxiety may be only a partial means of enabling him to learn and use more adaptive interpersonal and cognitive coping skills.

## DEFINING RELAXATION TRAINING

A number of counseling procedures are available to help a client lessen anxiety. Within the field of alcoholism treatment, these have included relaxation training, transcendental meditation, and biofeedback. There is not yet any evidence available to demonstrate that one of these techniques is more effective than the others with alcoholics. We will be emphasizing the use of relaxation training as it is derived from the principles of behavioral psychology. Biofeedback as it relates to inducing the relaxation response will also be described.

**Relaxation training** is a method of inducing deep muscular and cognitive relaxation. More emphasis is placed on muscular relaxation than is the case with transcendental meditation. Historically, relaxation training grew out of a method of deep muscle relaxation used by Dr. Edmund Jacobsen.[1] Later, Dr. Joseph Wolpe modified the procedure to treat anxiety related to specific clinical phenomena such as phobias.[2] He developed the modified procedure into a more global technique known as **systematic desensitization** in which anxiety-producing situations are repeatedly associated in imagination and in natural settings with muscular relaxation.

## USES OF RELAXATION TRAINING

Before discussing specific procedures for teaching relaxation, we will examine its uses with problem drinkers. Generally, relaxation training with problem drinkers can be used (1) to alleviate general anxiety and tension, (2) to relieve anxiety associated with specific social-emotional situations, (3) to reduce tension and restlessness prior to sleep, and (4) to control urges and cravings to drink.

Some individuals report generalized anxiety and tension throughout the day. This is especially true with alcoholics who have been detoxified, but are still experiencing mild anxiety. Rather than continuing the use of medications that might have been used in the detoxification process (such as minor tranquilizers which can be as physically addicting as alcohol), the counselor may choose to use relaxation training to enable the client to calm himself.

Relaxation training also is used to enable the client to cope more effectively with specific problem situations. A young female problem drinker may feel very anxious and upset when trying to discipline her children. This anxiety might interfere with her trying out more systematic child-rearing techniques that she has learned from the counselor. Relaxation training may lessen her anxiety enough so that she can at least attempt to implement new ways of responding to her children.

In another case, a heavy-drinking college student may be very passive and emotionally restricted. The counselor might use assertion training (refer to Chapter 5) to enable her to express her personal rights and feelings. However, after asserting herself with others, the client may feel unduly anxious and guilty about possibly hurting the other individual's feelings. Relaxation training and possibly systematic desensitization would be helpful in relieving this anxiety and would therefore increase the likelihood that the client would continue to use her newly learned assertiveness.

Many alcoholics suffer from chronic sleep disturbances. Some have so frequently used alcohol to help them get to sleep that they are unable to sleep when sober. Relaxation training has been found to be very useful with problems of insomnia. It can enable the client to lessen the cognitive and muscular tension that may be built up over the day.

Finally, relaxation training can help the client ward off urges to drink. After detoxification, urges to drink often recur for several weeks or months. The client can use relaxation training as one of several self-control procedures (refer to Chapter 8). Thus, the client learns to relax himself when urges occur or in situations that are likely to arouse urges or thoughts of alcohol.

## PROCEDURES FOR TEACHING RELAXATION
There are two basic procedures for training in deep muscle relaxation. The first was initially reported by Edmund Jacobsen (1968) and later popularized by Dr. Joseph Wolpe (1973). The second procedure is a newer but recently popularized technique known as biofeedback.

### Jacobsen-Wolpe Method
The method of *progressive relaxation* was initially reported by Dr. Edmund Jacobsen in the 1920's and 1930's. Dr. Jacobsen used this procedure to treat colitis and hypertension. In the 1950's, Dr. Wolpe shortened the procedure and successfully applied it to the treatment of phobias. The technique is now widely used, partly because of its simplicity and ease of administration.

The rationale for relaxation training and its uses, particularly as a self-control device, should be carefully explained to the client. Initial instructions usually include statements such as those which follow:

"I am going to teach you a procedure known as progressive relaxation, or deep muscle relaxation. Through this technique, you will be able to gain control over tension in your muscles and anxiety-producing thoughts. You will then be able to use this relaxation response to relieve yourself of anxiety when it arises or even to avoid anxiety before it occurs. By learning this relaxation, you will also be able to ward off urges to drink before they become too strong.

"Now, I would like you to sit comfortably in your chair. Even as you sit there in a relaxed position, there is a great deal of tension in your muscles. You are probably unaware of this tension. By systematically tensing and then relaxing various muscles in your body, you will be able to better recognize the tension state of your muscles and to control this tension. Some people become so adept at this skill that they are able to instantly relax themselves. With practice you may be able to do the same thing.

"One very important point is that the relaxation ability is a skill which can be developed through practice. You may have some difficulty at first, but with practice, you will find it easier and easier to relax. You will probably experience greater relaxation than you ever have before."

The instructions to the client should be positive and optimistic to take full advantage of placebo and expectancy factors in behavioral change. That is, if the client strongly believes (1) that he can learn the ability to completely relax and (2) that this skill will be effective in reducing anxiety, then the procedure will be more effective. Since the way the client develops this positive expectancy is through interactions with the counselor, the counselor must convey his own optimism and positive expectations regarding the procedure. Communicating this attitude to the client appears to be more a function of *how* the counselor describes the technique to the client rather than *what* words he uses. Counselors that are actively involved in the therapeutic interaction, interested in the client, effective, and enthusiastic can best accomplish this goal.

The basic procedure used by Jacobsen and Wolpe focuses on *muscle* relaxation. The client is seated in a comfortable position and systematically instructed to tense and then relax various muscle groups. While there does not appear to be any universally accepted sequence for administering this procedure, the counselor should develop some sequence to facilitate the learning process for the client. For example, muscle groups could be tensed and relaxed in this order: arms, head, neck, face, jaws, shoulders, back, chest, and legs.

Basically, the client is instructed to contract a particular muscle group and to experience the tense, tight feelings. Then she is to gradually relax that muscle group. She is instructed to concentrate on this "letting go" feeling and to experience the positive feelings of muscle tenseness being replaced by relaxation. Each muscle group is tensed and relaxed two or three times to allow the client to feel the difference between these two conditions in terms of bodily feedback and to become accustomed to letting the muscles become loose and limp. Training is usually spread over three to five sessions with each session lasting 30 to 60 minutes. Each session is spent on specific muscle groups. The arms and hands might be relaxed during the first session; the face, neck, head, and shoulders, during the second, and so on.

The following is a transcript of a relaxation session which will clarify the points just discussed.

"Now just sit back in your chair and try to be as comfortable as possible, and just try to relax as best as you can. Put your arms loosely on the sides of your chair, and concentrate on keeping your whole body very relaxed. Now, we are going to concentrate on your arm muscles today. I want you to first of all make a fist with your left hand . . . . Tighten that fist up as hard as you can . . . . Just tighten it up harder and harder . . . . You can feel the muscles in your forearm and in your upper arm getting tenser and tighter, and the muscles in your hand and your fingers are getting very tense and tight . . . . Now when you get really tense in that arm, I want you to slowly start to relax the muscle . . . . That's right, now . . . . Just start to relax the muscle . . . . Let your fingers and the muscles in your arm relax . . . and let that tension go . . . . Let that tension gradually fade away . . . . Concentrate on getting that arm muscle more and more relaxed . . . . Just let it get more and more relaxed . . . . That's it, just keep going with it . . . . That's fine . . . . Just keep relaxing it more and more . . . . Try to let it go . . . . Let the muscles go until your arm feels very relaxed and then rest it down on the chair. Now, I want you to try that again. Tense your arm again . . . . Make that fist . . . . Make it tense . . . . Now I want you to concentrate on that feeling of tenseness . . . . Concentrate on what that feels like in your arm . . . . Okay, now I want you to let it go . . . . Let your muscles start to relax . . . . Just let go . . .and concentrate on that feeling, what it feels like when it is all tensed up, and then as you start to let go of the muscle . . . how good it feels when you start to relax that muscle . . . . Let the muscle go . . . . Let it relax more and more . . . . The muscles in your fingers, and your hand, and in your forearm . . . . Let those muscles go . . . and just completely relax . . . . Let your arm fall on the chair and just get very loose and limp and relaxed.

"Now the other arm . . . . Take your other arm and make a fist . . . . Tense it up again as much as you can and get it tighter and tighter . . . . Tense it up tighter and tighter . . . . That's good . . . . Feel that tenseness . . . . Feel that tenseness in your arm . . . . Now start to relax and let your arm muscles go . . . . Feel that tension leave your hand and your fingers . . . . Feel it leaving . . . . Your hands are starting to feel relaxed . . . . You can feel that tension going. Just let it loose . . . . Let your arm loose . . . . Put it down on the chair . . . . Now, I want you to try that again . . . . Tense up that arm muscle again . . . . Get it tighter and tighter . . . . Concentrate on what that feels like . . . and then start to relax . . . . Just as you are able to tense that muscle up as much as you want to, you also are able to loosen it and relax it as much as you want. It is completely within your power to do that . . . . Let it loose, let your arm muscle relax . . . . Just let it happen . . . . Let it relax, let your muscle tense out, stretch your arm out a bit . . . . Let your arm down on the chair . . . and then just get it completely relaxed . . . . Very good. Now we are going to work on your upper arms some more, around your biceps . . . . I want you to put your arm on the chair with your palm down. I am going to put my hand on your wrist, and I want you to push up against my hand with your wrist . . . . Just put pressure on my hand with your wrist . . . . Then notice that muscles in your forearm and in your upper arm are getting tense . . . . Tense that up, press up against my hand, that's good . . . . That's it now, let it go, just let your arm down again and you can feel your arm relax . . . . Feel those muscles getting relaxed . . . . Concentrate on just letting it go more and more . . . . That's it . . . . Now try that one more time . . . . Lift up your arm again . . . . Push up against my hand, and feel the tenseness . . . . Concentrate on the tenseness now . . . . Let it go . . . . Let your arm relax . . . and let it go further this time than you did before . . . . Let it go loose and limp . . . . That's it . . . . Just let it go loose and limp . . . completely relaxed . . . more and more. Now it may seem very relaxed, now I want you to go even further . . . . Let it go even further and further again . . . . Just as you are able to tense it, I also want you to relax it . . . . Now let's try it with that same arm pushed down against the chair . . . . Just put it down as hard as you can . . . . With your wrist . . . . Push your wrist down against the chair and you can feel the muscles in the upper part of your arm and your forearm tense up . . . . That's good . . . now relax and just get more and more relaxed. Very good. Now let's try the other arm. I am going to put my hand on the wrist of your other arm . . . . Push your arm . . . . Push your wrist up against my hand . . . . Push up . . . . That's it . . . . Get that arm tense . . . . Okay . . . . Now let it go . . . . Let it relax . . . more and more . . . . Let that tenseness go . . . . Very good . . . . Now push down with your wrist against the chair and tense up those muscles . . . . Now let it go . . . . Let your arm muscle relax more and more . . . . Concentrate on the relaxation. You are doing fine. Now, I'd like you to try to get more comfortable in the chair . . . . Put your arms on the sides of the chair and get your arms very comfortable . . . . Close your eyes . . . . Close your eyes and concentrate . . . . Just concentrate on the arm muscles . . . . Okay, just try to get more and more relaxed . . . . Let them go loose and limp . . . . Try to get the feeling you did just as you let go of the tension before . . . and your arm muscles started to gradually relax . . . . Let that happen again . . . . Let the arm muscle get relaxed and let your arms go now. That's good. You'll be feeling more relaxed. Your arms will start to feel different now . . . . When people start to get relaxed in their muscles, they get a different sensation in their muscles . . . . You may notice that your muscles in your arms become very loose and limp and you may feel a kind of numbness in your arms . . . . You may feel either a heavy or light sensation . . . or a warm sensation . . . . You may feel various kinds of things but when your arms are starting to feel different, as I have described, you will know that you are getting relaxed. Now keep concentrating on the relaxation in your muscles . . . . Now even though the muscles in your arms are very relaxed right now, I want you to try to get them even more so . . . . Just let them go . . . even more . . . . Concentrate on the different feelings that you are having in your arms . . . and try to expand that and try to get that feeling to increase . . . . Let the relaxation develop . . . . You have the control of your muscles . . . . All you have to do is let it happen . . . . Just let them go . . . . Let them relax more and more."

Subsequent sessions would then be spent concentrating on the rest of the muscles in the body. The general procedure would be similar for each with only the methods for tensing muscle groups differing. These methods are presented below.

*Hands and arms.* As indicated in the transcript, the client is instructed to "make a fist," first with one hand and then the other. The client is then told to rest her arm (the palm of the hand should be facing downward) comfortably on the chair. The counselor places his hand firmly on the client's wrist and instructs the client to push up with her wrist against his hand. Finally, the client is instructed to push down against the chair with her wrist, without the aid of the counselor.

*Neck.* The client is instructed to turn her head to the right as far as possible, stretching the neck muscles. This is then repeated in the other direction, turning the head to the left. The client is then told to bring her head "all the way back, trying to touch your upper back with the back of your head." The head is then lowered to the front with the client trying to touch her chest with her chin.

*Face and jaw.* There are a number of small muscle groups in the face which are particularly important with clients who complain of tension headaches. Ways of tensing these muscles include pursing the lips, furrowing the brow, smiling in an exaggerated fashion, and frowning. Relaxing the jaw muscles also is essential particularly with individuals who characteristically grit their teeth when they are angry or anxious. In fact, gritting the teeth is exactly the way clients are instructed to tense their jaw muscles. It is important to remember that to completely relax the jaw muscles after tensing them, the mouth must be opened slightly.

*Shoulders and back.* The client is instructed to shrug her shoulders as if trying to touch her ears with them. To tense the back muscles, the client is asked to arch her back and to push her shoulders back as if trying to touch them together.

*Legs.* The leg muscles are contracted in much the same way as the arm muscles were. Initially, the legs should be stretched out straight, either on a couch or a lounge chair. The counselor places his hand on the client's ankle and instructs her to "push up against my hand with as much force as you can." The ankle is then pushed down forcefully against the chair or couch.

*Chest and diaphragm.* To relax and tense muscles in the chest area, clients are instructed to take a deep breath, hold it for a few seconds, and then slowly exhale. This is repeated two to three times.

Periodically, throughout the relaxation sessions, the counselor will want to assess the client's relaxation response. This can be accomplished in two ways. The first and most practical way for most counselors is a self-rating scale ranging from 0 to 10 or 0 to 100. The zero point of the scale is usually "the most calm and relaxed you have ever felt" with the highest point of the scale indicating "the most anxious and tense you have ever felt." The client can be asked prior to, during, and near the end of each relaxation session to rate herself on this scale.

Another, more complex, method of assessment is through **electromyography**. This physiological assessment procedure measures muscle activity, usually via electrodes attached to the frontalis muscles of the forehead. Ordinarily, this more sophisticated evaluation system is used only when relaxation training is being combined with electromyogram (EMG) biofeedback to induce muscle relaxation.

## Electromyogram (EMG) Biofeedback

It has been postulated by some proponents of the clinical applications of biofeedback procedures that electromyogram (EMG) feedback will enhance the ability of clients to attain deep levels of muscle relaxation. Essentially, this procedure entails providing the client with immediate information on muscle activity during the relaxation session. The client is supposedly able to maintain better control over muscle tension with the aid of this information. Unfortunately, reviews[3] of controlled scientific studies of EMG biofeedback indicate that this procedure does not add significantly to the Jacobsen-Wolpe relaxation method in terms of assisting clients in achieving muscle relaxation. The same is true of other forms of biofeedback such as alpha-wave conditioning. In spite of these findings, biofeedback procedures are becoming popular in alcoholism treatment. Counselors too often are seduced by novel therapeutic approaches accompanied by unsubstantiated claims of therapeutic success. Often such success cases are more a function of the enthusiasm of the counselor and client and the placebo effects associated with the biofeedback gadgetry than of the procedure itself. The counselor is doing both himself and his clients a disservice by not closely evaluating the clinical research literature on the effectiveness of new treatment procedures.

## Cognitive Aspects Of Relaxation Training

In addition to tensing and relaxing specific muscle groups, relaxation also can be enhanced through various cognitive procedures. For example, during muscle relaxation training, clients often are instructed to think of the word "calm" or "relax." The client is told to picture one of these words vividly in his mind and to concentrate on it. This procedure accomplishes two goals. First, by concentrating on one specific image, the client lessens the likelihood of anxiety related to intrusive thoughts which might interfere with the relaxation response. Second, by repeatedly associating specific key words ("calm") with the relaxation response, the word itself can be used by the client as a cue for the response. Some clients can become so adept at relaxing that the mental image of the word "relax" or "calm" will result in muscle relaxation. It will at least serve as a cue for the client to become more aware of his current state of muscle tension.

Thoughts of certain experiences also can enhance the relaxation response. The counselor can describe a situation and instruct the client to imagine the scene vividly, using all of his senses. That is, the client should attempt to see, hear, feel, and smell everything being described. Scenes should relate to experiences which the client describes as being positive, but not emotionally arousing. An example scene follows:

"You are walking slowly through a wooded area. There are tall trees all around you. You're walking on a path next to a small, shallow, babbling brook. You can hear the water in the brook running over stones on the bottom. You keep walking very slowly. You look up and see the sun shining through the trees. You also see and hear birds in the trees. You can hear them singing very clearly.

"As you walk further, you come to the end of the woods. You see a large meadow in front of you. The sun is shining very brightly. As you walk along, you can feel the warmth of the sun against your face. There is also a soft breeze which you can feel on your skin.

"You walk toward a huge oak tree in the middle of the meadow. You walk very slowly, feeling very calm and relaxed. You don't have a care in the world.

"When you get to the tree, you lie down underneath it. The grass is surprisingly soft. You feel as though you're lying on a cloud. You look up through the tree and notice how blue the sky looks. Birds are singing and there are just a few white fluffy clouds against the blue sky. You are completely relaxed. You feel very warm and comfortable."

### Homework Assignments

The client is provided with specific homework assignments to help maintain the relaxation response in the natural environment. Clients are instructed to practice the skills they have learned during relaxation training sessions at least three times per week for 15 to 20 minutes each time. They should choose a quiet location at home, preferably at a time when they will not be bothered by others.

Clients should be encouraged to begin to put their relaxation abilities into practice by using them to prevent or to cope with anxiety in their everyday life. Findings show the relaxation response is very helpful with clients who suffer from tension headaches or insomnia. When a headache occurs before bedtime, the client should lie down and concentrate on deep muscle relaxation for 15 to 30 minutes. Clients with headaches should pay particular attention to relaxing the muscles in the head, face, and neck.

Basically, the client must learn to use relaxation in a self-control manner. It is effective only in relation to its use by the client.

58

## SYSTEMATIC DESENSITIZATION

To deal with more specific anxiety problems, relaxation training frequently is combined with **systematic desensitization**. This procedure involves the gradual association between relaxation and images of anxiety-producing situations, presented in a hierarchical order. Systematic desensitization was originally developed as a treatment for individuals with specific phobias (i.e., an unrealistic fear of a person, place, object, animal, or situation—such as a fear of heights). *The rationale of the procedure is that fears will diminish if they are repeatedly experienced and associated with a feeling of relaxation both in imagination and eventually in real life.* This technique is useful with clients who are having difficulty (1) in using the relaxation response as a self-control device in their everyday life due to extreme anxiety and (2) in implementing new assertiveness or social-learning skills in interpersonal situations due to severe anxiety and apprehension.

Prior to systematic desensitization, the counselor assists the client in devising a hierarchical list of situations within one general category that causes anxiety. For example, if a client reports anxiety in relation to socializing with groups of people, heterosexual interactions, and authority figures at work, a separate list would be generated for each of these categories. Situations should be rank-ordered from those producing the least anxiety near the bottom of the list to those producing the most anxiety near the top. Table 6 shows two example lists—one for general interpersonal anxiety and the other for a more specific airplane phobia.

These lists must be long enough so that they are gradual in terms of anxiety; large "jumps" in anxiety in the list could interfere with a smooth progression through it.

After the list(s) is complete, the counselor teaches the client progressive muscle relaxation as described previously. Then, while relaxed, the client is instructed to imagine (in vivid detail, using all of her senses) the item producing least anxiety (the counselor starts at the bottom of the list and works up). The client is told to continue to relax while thinking of the situation. If the client begins to feel anxious, she is instructed to raise her index finger to indicate this feeling to the counselor. The counselor then instructs the client to immediately discontinue thinking about the scene and try to relax once again. This procedure is repeated until the client can imagine the scene for a period of time (perhaps a minute) without experiencing anxiety. The scene is often repeated two to three times even after the client is able to relax while imagining it. Each scene on the list is presented in this manner until the client can imagine all of the situations while remaining re-

## TABLE 6.  SAMPLE SYSTEMATIC DESENSITIZATION HIERARCHIES

*Interpersonal Anxiety Hierarchy*

A social gathering of 25 people at which you know only the host. As you walk in, everyone turns to look at you.

A social gathering of 25 people at which you know most of them fairly well.

A social gathering of 15 people being held at your friend's house. You know all but a few people.

A social gathering of five people at your friend's house. You know all of the people, except one.

A gathering of two friends and yourself at their house.

You and your best friend are together at his house.

You and your best friend are together at your house.

*Plane Phobia Hierarchy*

Airplane flying in the air.

Airplane lifting off the ground.

Airplane beginning take-off.

Airplane stopping, ready for take-off.

Airplane taxiing on runway.

Stewardess announcing safety precautions.

Engines starting.

Sitting in airplane.

Entering airplane.

Walking up ramp to airplane.

Checking ticket at last gate.

Hearing announcement of airplane departure.

Checking in at ticket desk.

In your car, driving to the airport.

At home, two hours before departure.

laxed. Systematic desensitization may last from one to several sessions, depending on the client's progress.

The next step is to generalize these results to the real world. The way of accomplishing this goal is to establish a hierarchical list of real-life situations that the client will probably be engaging in over the next several weeks. In some cases (e.g., when a client has difficulty in initiating interactions with others), the client may be instructed to arrange for events to occur in a hierarchical order during a week. For example:

1. Ask Joan R. for a date.
2. Ask Joan R. to lunch.
3. Talk to Joan R. about mutual interests.
4. Ask Joan R. a question.
5. Say "hello" to Joan R.

Prior to and during each situation, the client can concentrate on relaxation. It is often helpful for the client to rehearse the situation in imagination, while relaxing, prior to its occurrence. After the client successfully completes this assignment, he is encouraged to use both progressive muscle relaxation and systematic desensitization as self-control procedures to deal with future anxiety problems.

## RELAXATION AS A SELF-CONTROL TECHNIQUE

Recent studies indicate that relaxation training is most effective when the relaxation response is used as a self-control technique. As earlier mentioned, there is nothing automatic or magical about relaxation training. In a sense, the usefulness of relaxation training begins *after* training is complete.

Bob W. is a 33-year-old business executive who has recently been promoted in his company. His new promotion to district sales manager has brought with it a number of new problems. In his new position, Bob is expected to present periodic talks to his salesmen and make speeches at regional and national meetings. Bob has always been unsure of himself in public, particularly when he is presenting a talk. While he has had a significant drinking problem in the past, he has recently (with the help of a psychologist) been able to refrain from drinking. Responsibilities of his promotion, however, are a serious threat to his sobriety.

Bob's counselor suggests the use of relaxation training to help Bob deal with his anxiety. Actually, Bob's anxiety is most prominent prior to a public speech. In fact, he begins to feel anxious while driving to work on the morning of his speech, with his anxiety slowly increasing throughout the day. Just before his talk, he usually experiences rapid heart palpitations, sweating, nausea, and at times, diarrhea. Once his speech begins, however, Bob's anxiety gradually subsides. Bob is actually quite good at speeches, presenting a good image to his audience. He normally is well prepared and has an effective delivery.

Over four sessions, Bob's psychologist teaches him deep muscle relaxation. Bob practices this relaxation response every day between therapy sessions. The psychologist provides Bob with an audiotape of one of the training sessions to assist him in his practice sessions at home.

Prior to his next scheduled speech, Bob is instructed to play the relaxation training tape in his car on the way to the talk. He is to concentrate on relaxing. When he arrives at the speaking engagement, he is to maintain his concentration on muscle relaxation while conversing with his salesmen. Approximately 30 minutes prior to his talk, he is to excuse himself, saying that he wants to look over his notes. He is to find a secluded spot and practice relaxing for 15 to 20 minutes. Bob also can use his relaxation training to suppress urges to drink triggered by his anxiety.

In this case, Bob is acting as his own counselor by implementing relaxation to alleviate anxiety as the need arises.

## Footnotes

1. E. Jacobsen. *Progressive relaxation.* Chicago: University of Chicago Press, 1968.

2. J. Wolpe. *The practice of behavior therapy.* New York: Pergamon Press, Inc., 1973.

3. E. B. Blanchard and L. D. Young. Clinical applications of biofeedback training: A review of evidence. *Archives of General Psychiatry, 30,* 573-589.

# 5  Assertion Training

## DEFINING ASSERTIVENESS

A great many alcoholics have marked deficiencies in social-emotional skills. That is, they have difficulty in their relationships with other people, particularly in terms of emotional expression. We often refer to the use of these particular skills as **assertiveness**. Assertive behavior refers to the skills necessary to *appropriately* express personal rights and feelings. This might include the ability to say "no" to someone, to disagree with another person, to express an unpopular opinion in a group, to express anger or dissatisfaction, or to provide constructive feedback to others. These examples involve *negative* emotion. Assertiveness also refers to the expression of *positive* thoughts and feelings. One should be able, without undue anxiety, to express feelings of love and caring, to compliment another person, or to provide positive feedback to others ("When you say things like that, it makes me feel very close to you").

On the assertiveness dimension, an individual can be either too passive and dependent or too explosive and hostile. Either extreme is a demonstration of a *lack* of assertiveness. Many people confuse assertiveness with aggressiveness. Assertiveness is the appropriate expression of rights and feelings with its appropriateness being judged by three criteria. These consist of whether or not the interpersonal response (1) leads to desired results (e.g., results in a positive change in another individual's behavior), (2) is relatively satisfying to the individual being assertive and (3) is relatively satisfying to the interpersonal partner (i.e., the target of the assertiveness). For example, a bully could satisfy Criteria 1 and 2 via physical threats and abuse. Such aggressiveness, however, is not likely to be satisfying to others, so Criterion 3 would not be satisfied. On the other hand, suppose that an attractive female engaged in seductive and coy maneuvers to "assert" herself with a male friend. She might accomplish her goal (Criterion 1), and her response might be considered relatively satisfactory by her friend (Criterion 3). However, she may find such coyness personally distasteful and want to learn to respond to others in a more direct manner.

## ALCOHOL ABUSE AND ASSERTIVENESS

Numerous behavioral studies have demonstrated a direct relationship between deficits in assertiveness and excessive alcohol consumption. Deficiencies in assertiveness often serve as cues for heavy drinking. Alcohol abuse can lead to a reduction in anxiety about such personal deficiencies, a reduction in the pent-up anger associated with the lack of assertiveness (often in the form of an "I-don't-give-a-damn" attitude), and an increased repertoire of social-emotional behaviors that result in the expression of feelings. Thus, we observe the individual who is normally inhibited and docile become hostile, belligerent, and verbally abusive when intoxicated. This valiant attempt at assertiveness is typically an utter failure. On the other hand, we find the individual who is normally quiet, reserved, and shy who becomes friendly, outgoing, and emotionally expressive when inebriated. *The theory behind assertion training with alcoholics is that if an individual were to learn ways to cope with troublesome social-emotional situations appropriately, there would be no need for excessive drinking.* The counselor would be providing an *alternative* to alcohol abuse that not only solves the immediate interpersonal problem more efficiently but also has a number of beneficial side effects. Subsequent to successful assertion training, clients often report increases in self-esteem, feelings of social competence, and feelings of self-worth. In addition, friends and relatives begin to develop a healthy respect for the client. In fact, those who are the "target" of his assertiveness are the ones who learn to respect him most.

Assertiveness, as a problem-solving device, not only serves as an alternative behavior but also serves as a behavior that is incompatible with excessive drinking. Research has indicated that, when confronted with a stressful interpersonal situation requiring assertiveness, normal social drinkers prefer either not to drink alcohol or to drink very little. Alcoholics will drink extensively under these conditions. It seems as though the social drinkers realize (or perhaps have learned through past experience) that it is difficult to be effective in stressful interpersonal situations and intoxicated at the same time. In a sense they have learned that drinking and their ability to respond assertively are incompatible so that the former actually prevents the latter.

## COMPONENTS OF ASSERTIVENESS

As might be expected, the definition of assertiveness is not simple. What makes one verbal interaction assertive and another one not assertive is, at times, difficult to determine. Recently, the behavioral components of assertiveness have been determined by comparing the nature of responses of individuals rated as being high in assertion with those rated as being low in assertion. These analyses have indicated that an assertive response is composed of a variety of specific verbal and nonverbal behaviors. The most essential verbal components include the following:

1. *Speech duration:* Assertive responses are longer than nonassertive ones.
2. *Loudness:* Assertive responses are loud, with a firm tone.
3. *Noncompliance:* The nature of the verbal response is such that the client does not give in by agreeing with something that she really does not want to agree with (e.g., saying yes to an unreasonable demand when she really wants to refuse).
4. *Request for behavior change:* An assertive response includes a statement that would rectify a difficult situation not only in the present (e.g., "I ordered a rare steak and this one is well done. Please take this one back and bring me what I ordered") but also in the future (e.g., "Please don't *ever* ask me to have a drink with you again because I've quit for good").

The most essential nonverbal components (which are often as important or even more important than the verbal ones) include the following:

1. *Affect:* Assertive responses have more meaning or emotional involvement which is expressed via facial expressions, tone of voice, and/or hand and arm gestures. Nonassertive responses are typically accompanied by smiles, rigid posturing, and a weak voice.
2. *Eye contact:* When a person is being assertive, the eyes must be focused directly on the other person. Nonassertive responders often avoid eye contact, tending to look away from others.

The identification of these components has enabled clinicians to more easily teach assertiveness. Specific deficits are much easier to pinpoint. It must be noted that not all clients will exhibit each of these deficits. Some will be able to speak loudly and to look the person in the eyes but will not be able to request a behavior change. Not all clients will need to be taught all components. Thus, to save the clinician's and client's time, a careful analysis of each client's deficits is necessary.

## ASSESSMENT AND SELECTION
## OF PROBLEM SITUATIONS

Initially, the counselor must focus on two areas: (1) the assessment of situations calling for assertiveness that lead to alcohol abuse and (2) the assessment of the client's behavior in these situations. In essence, these areas are investigated to determine if assertion training is necessary. Both of these assessment strategies were discussed at some length in Chapter 2. Methods of assessment for assertive behaviors, however, will be briefly described here.

### Interviewing In Assessment

One of the most direct and easiest methods of gathering evaluation information is interviewing the client. This not only provides a source of descriptive data but also a means whereby the counselor can observe the client's behavior. Does the client behave passively or assertively with the counselor? Is there a marked verbal-behavioral discrepancy; i.e., does the client describe herself in one way but appear to be very different?

### Self-Report And Its Evaluation

This discrepancy is often quite evident when the client completes self-rated behavioral inventories. For example, the Wolpe-Lazarus Inventory[1] and Rathus Assertiveness Scale[2] are assertiveness questionnaires that can be completed by clients as part of the initial evaluation. However, the counselor must be very careful in evaluating this self-reported information. Clinical research studies indicate that alcoholics, as compared to clients with other types of problems, describe themselves as being much *more* assertive than they actually are. This is particularly true when negative assertiveness is being assessed. There is less of a discrepancy for positive assertiveness. Thus, if the necessity for assertion training were judged simply on questionnaires, it might look as though none of the alcoholic clients lacked assertiveness. In addition, alcoholics often are adept at knowing what to do or say in a problem situation, but being unable to do it. For example:

John W.'s drinking problem seems very much related to conflict with others whom he cannot get along with. His major problem is a lack of assertiveness. However, on the basis of questionnaires and interviews, he appears to be a very self-assured, assertive individual. When asked to describe a confrontation with his boss, John explains, "Yes, I really told him what I had on my mind! I believe that he respected me for my opinions on the bank deal even though I essentially disagreed with his position." In reality, John behaved very sheepishly with his boss and, even though he strongly disagreed with him, said nothing. How is the counselor to obtain a true picture of the client?

*Checking self-report through role playing.* There are several methods of dealing with the question of whether or not the client is trying to "con" the counselor. John can be requested to *show* exactly how he interacted with his boss. The situation can be re-enacted through role playing, with the counselor playing the part of the boss and John being himself. The counselor should initially obtain a detailed description of the boss from John so that he can simulate the real encounter as closely as possible. The idea is to enable John to experience the same feelings and attitudes that he has in the presence of his boss. John may be extremely hesitant to role play the scene. Most people are a bit anxious about role playing. In a sense, the counselor is not only evaluating John with this procedure but also he is confronting him with the realities of his behavior. John is encouraged to play the part as if it were really happening. Many clients have a tendency to explain or describe their responses, "If I were in this situation, I would say . . . . .", or "If he said that to me, I would really give him a piece of my mind." The counselor should insist on active role playing.

A client who was treated by one of the authors abided by these instructions *literally*. When role playing a marital scene with a female treatment assistant, the client got up and walked out of the room in response to the role model's statement about a problem with the children. When asked to explain his behavior, he replied, "You told me to respond as I would in real life. When my wife makes a statement that I disagree with, I simply walk out of the room!" His compulsive compliance with the counselor's instructions provided an important bit of information on exactly what occurs in the home.

When the client role plays the problem situation, the counselor can directly observe the person's assertiveness as related to the components described earlier. If a client is not able to respond assertively *outside* the counseling session, it is not likely that she will be able to respond differently in the presence of the counselor. Once role playing begins, the client usually becomes so involved in the situation that she responds as she normally would.

Another way to assess a client is to expose her to a series of more structured role-played social situations that the counselor suspects are difficult for her or that the client has described as difficult. Typically, the client is requested to role play a wide variety of scenes. Variety is necessary since assertiveness *per se* is not a global personality trait that one either has or does not have. Rather, an individual's assertiveness varies from situation to situation. Certainly, we may observe some general patterns, such as the lack of assertiveness only with certain types of individuals, e.g., authority figures.

It is helpful to examine the client's assertive responses in scenes in which the role model assumes the role of both familiar (spouse) and unfamiliar (salesperson) individuals and both male and female respondents. In addition, scenes should be related to interpersonal, marital, employment, parent-child, and drinking relationships.

It is often less anxiety producing for the client to begin with a standard series of scenes that might be applicable to anyone. Such a series is the *Behavioral Assertiveness Test* (BAT) devised by Dr. Richard Eisler and his colleagues.[3] This series includes the following scenes:*

> 1. Narrator: You have just come home from work, and as you settle down to read the newspaper you discover that your wife has cut out an important article in order to get a recipe that is on the back of it. You really like to read the whole newspaper. Role Model Wife: I just wanted to cut out a recipe before I forgot about it.
>
> 2. Narrator: You have just punished your son for his inconsiderate behavior and told him that he must stay in his room for the rest of the afternoon. Your wife feels sorry for him and tells him that he can go out to play. Role Model Wife: It's so nice outside; it's a shame to make him stay in his room.
>
> 3. Narrator: You come home late one night, and your wife demands an explanation of why you are so late. As soon as you begin to explain, she interrupts you and starts screaming about how inconsiderate you are. Role Model Wife: I don't care what happened. You are the most inconsiderate person in the world for making me worry about you.
>
> 4. Narrator: You have just bought a new shotgun, the one you've always wanted. Role Model Wife: You didn't need another shotgun. You have too many now.
>
> 5. Narrator: You have just come home from a hard day's work hoping to have a nice home-cooked meal. Instead you find that your wife has another frozen T.V.

*Reprinted with permission from R. M. Eisler, P. M. Miller, and M. Hersen. Components of assertive behavior. *Journal of Clinical Psychology*, 1973, *29*, 295-299.

dinner in the oven. Role Model Wife: I didn't have time to cook again today. I hope you don't mind having a frozen dinner.

6. Narrator: Your wife has just told you that she just has to have another chair for the living room. You know that you can't afford it. Role Model Wife: Please let's order the chair now. You promised we could have it.

7. Narrator: You're in the middle of an exciting football game. Your wife walks in and changes the T.V. channel as she does every time you're watching a good game. Role Model Wife: Let's watch this movie instead; it's supposed to be real good.

8. Narrator: You've just put up a new shelf in the kitchen which has taken you some time to put together. Your wife comes in and makes some critical comments to the effect that you're not a very good carpenter. Role Model Wife: Would you mind taking that awful-looking shelf down.

9. Narrator: Your wife proudly presents you with a shirt she has bought you for your birthday. You don't like the color and would like to exchange it for another, but you don't want to hurt her feelings. Role Model Wife: Here's your birthday present. I hope you like it.

10. Narrator: You have just come home from a hard day's work dead tired. Your wife informs you that she has accepted an invitation for you both to visit some friends that evening. You're definitely not in the mood to go out. Role Model Wife: I just knew that you'd like to visit tonight; let's go right after dinner.

11. Narrator: You're in a crowded grocery store and are in a hurry. You've picked up one small item and get in line to pay for it when a woman with a shopping cart full of groceries cuts in line right in front of you. Role Model Woman: You won't mind if I cut in here, will you? I'm late for an appointment.

12. Narrator: You're in a drug store, and you buy something that costs 75 cents. You go to the cashier to pay for it and hand her a five-dollar bill. She rings up the sale and hands you 25 cents, change for only a dollar. Role Model Cashier: Here's your change, sir.

13. Narrator: You have just bought a new shirt and upon

putting it on for the first time, noticed that several buttons are missing. You return to the sales clerk who sold it to you. Role Model Sales Clerk: May I help you sir?

14. Narrator: You're in a restaurant with some friends. You order a very rare steak. The waitress brings a steak to the table which is so well done it looks burned. Role Model Waitress: I hope you enjoy your dinner sir.

*Checking self-report through other observers.* One final method of obtaining information on the client's assertiveness is to request both she and her friends or relatives to keep a written record or **behavioral diary** of actual occurrences of interpersonal situations requiring assertiveness. Thus, each time the client is involved in such a situation in real life, both she and those observing or involved in the encounter would immediately write down the nature of the situation, the specific verbal behavior of both persons involved, specific feelings (e.g., anxieties), and the outcome. In fact, it is helpful to request that these observations be recorded continuously throughout the counseling process to provide an ongoing record of progress. These records also provide the client with feedback on her performance which, in turn, motivates her to further implement what is learned in assertion training.

## PREPARING THE CLIENT

Preparation of the client is as important in assertion training as it is in any therapeutic endeavor. Although it is essential, adequate preparation is frequently overlooked or minimized. In fact, when one reads the clinical research literature on assertion training, it appears that the procedure is a very direct and simple one to which all clients readily submit themselves. This is not true. Many clients are wary of assertion training and have misconceptions about it.

The first problem facing the counselor is to discuss with the client his lack of assertiveness and the relationship of this deficit to excessive drinking. Alcoholics often are defensive about their deficiencies and initially may deny problems in this area. A combined approach of gentle persuasion and empathetic confrontation usually helps the client admit to his difficulties. For example, the counselor can point out the number of past situations which required assertive responding and eventually led to drinking. The client may tend to blame the responses of others rather than his own deficiencies. It may help to try reverse role playing with clients to demonstrate the effects of their behavior on others and on themselves. The following example illustrates this point.

Harry Y. is a 39-year-old married man whose heavy drinking

usually follows explosive arguments with others. Harry's way of dealing with others is to be either extremely passive and dependent or to become enraged and to have an "adult temper tantrum." Subsequent to his tantrums, Harry becomes despondent, feeling that nobody really likes him. When his counselor discussed the possibility of assertion training, Harry emphatically denied his need for such treatment. He explained that other people were to blame for his explosive outbursts and even though he tried to be nice to people, they just did not like him. The counselor suggested they role play the last encounter that Harry had with his wife. Harry would play the part of his wife and the counselor would play Harry.

| *Wife (Harry)* | *Harry (Counselor)* |
|---|---|
| Harry, we've got to make some decisions about being more consistent in disciplining our children. | (Silence) |
| Harry, did you hear me? | (Silence, sneering at wife) |
| Harry, we can't avoid this issue any longer. | I'll go along with whatever you say. We always end up doing things your way anyway (Sarcastically). |
| Well, suggest something. | Okay, let's start by your telling me what I need to do differently with the children. |
| (In a mild tone of voice) Alright Harry, to be honest with you, I think you're too hard on the children sometimes. You either ignore them or you're losing your temper with them. | (Enraged) Damn it! Why am I the one who's always wrong. I suppose you're perfect. You're just a no-good bitch and I should have never married you. You either complain about my drinking or the way I deal with the kids. (Yelling). You're too damn lenient with those kids. You let them get away with murder! |

During this role-played sequence, the counselor consciously exaggerated Harry's usual responses. By playing his wife's part and observing his own reactions (as portrayed by the counselor), Harry can begin to recognize his interpersonal deficiencies. The counselor can analyze the scene with Harry, pointing out his initial lack of assertiveness when his wife wanted to discuss a mutual problem. Harry may point out that he felt very anxious and intimidated by his wife. The counselor might also demonstrate the relationship between Harry's initial lack of response and his wife's escalation of her insistence for his reply. Finally, the counselor can discuss the effects of Harry's outburst and some alternative assertive responses which might have solved the problem more efficiently.

Occasionally, clients perceive assertiveness as an undesirable trait. They claim that one should "turn the other cheek" and should be nice to others. Often this objection is related to a basic misunderstanding regarding the nature of assertive behavior. The client is confusing assertiveness with aggressiveness or rudeness. In this case, the counselor must describe in more detail what is meant by assertiveness. Emphasis should be placed on descriptions of open expressions of both positive and negative feelings without being passive or aggressive. Numerous examples in which the counselor describes an assertive, aggressive, and a passive response to the same situation are helpful. For example:

A friend has borrowed a very valuable book that was given to you by your grandmother. The friend had promised to return the book last week, but you still have not received it. You need the book this week. The friend calls you on the phone and, during the conversation, mentions that she has loaned the book to one of her neighbors.

*Passive response:* Oh, well . . . er . . . a, I hope she likes it.

*Aggressive response:* What!! You had no right to loan my book to her! If I don't have that book back within one hour, I'm going to call the police!!

*Assertive response:* I really needed that book back this week. It's very valuable to me and I wish you wouldn't have loaned it to someone without asking me first. Please ask your friend to return the book to you at once. I would like you to return it to me by this afternoon.

The counselor can demonstrate the negative effects of both the passive and the aggressive response in terms of (1) the end result of getting the book back, (2) anxiety and tension elicited by a passive response, (3) lack of respect from others, (4) future occurrences of the same individual taking advantage of similar situations and (5) the possibility of the client's drinking as a result of her inadequate way of handling the problem.

Some clients are hesitant about assertion training because they perceive the process as being too artificial. They feel, even if they learn to act assertively with the counselors, they will never be able to change their behavior in real life. The counselor should be honest and agree that role playing is likely to be very artificial at first. As the client practices and learns to be more adept at assertiveness, however, role playing will become natural. Often these rational arguments against assertion training actually are related to a high degree of anxiety about role playing and about behavior change.

In regard to the preparation of the client for assertion training, the counselor must keep two major points in mind: (1) unless the client is actively cooperative and at least minimally committed to behavior change, assertion training will be of little benefit, and (2) the goal with hesitant or anxious clients should be to at least involve them in one session of assertion training so that they can alleviate their fears about the procedure.

The counselor should explain to the client the rationale behind assertion training and a step-by-step analysis of the technique as it will be applied to her.

One final problem often encountered is the client's unrealistic perceptions about the effects of assertiveness. Many clients report fears of being disliked, rejected, or physically attacked if they behave assertively. When these fears occur, cognitive retraining as described in Chapter 8 or relaxation training as described in Chapter 4 are useful in alleviating these fears.

## ELEMENTS OF TRAINING

### Role Playing Procedures

Once the assertion scenes are selected and the client is prepared, assertion training can proceed. Typed on an index card, each scene includes a verbal prompt by the role model to initiate the interaction (e.g., "Well, Sarah, what do you think of my idea?"). Scenes are arranged in a hierarchical order so that those likely to produce the least anxiety for the client are role played first. As in the assessment phase, the counselor should enlist the aid of colleagues as role models for the scenes. During assessment, the counselor should have obtained a sample of those components of assertiveness that will require the most training. Training is most efficient when one or two components common to several scenes are taught at a time, rather than when all components for one scene are taught before proceeding to the other scenes. Thus, the client might learn eye contact and loudness for each scene before other components are taught. The sequence of teaching components varies with the individual client's needs although, as a rule, the verbal components are taught before the nonverbal ones.

Teaching techniques that should be used in training follow.

*Instruction.* Probably the most elementary, but often most effective, teaching technique consists of specific instructions to the client on what is expected of him. Thus, the counselor may say, "Okay, now, in the next scenes I want you to concentrate on looking directly at Joan when you reply. Remember: look directly at her when you speak." Instructions must be very specific and must be repeated frequently (e.g., before each scene). It is often helpful to request the client to repeat instructions to insure that he understands what is expected.

*Modeling.* **Modeling** refers to providing an example for the client. After instructing the client, the counselor should role play the scene, demonstrating the desired response. Modeling is particularly important when teaching the more complex components of assertiveness, such as affect. Either before or after modeling, the counselor can point out specific aspects of her behavior so that the client can focus his attention on them. For example, she may say, "John, did you notice how I moved my arms and the expression on my face? I'll model that once more and you watch closely."

Sometimes an assistant can serve as the role model. For example, it often is more productive to enlist the aid of other counselors, secretarial personnel, or volunteers since the scenes may require varied ages, sex, and demeanors on the part of the role model. This also allows the counselor to observe and take notes on the client's behavior.

*A major assumption of the modeling technique is that the counselor or other role model is able to provide a good example of assertiveness.* Some counselors may require practice of these components before engaging in assertion training with clients. Feedback can be provided either by colleagues or via video or audiotaping.

Videotaping or at least audiotaping should also be used with the client. Taping the scenes allows the counselor to (1) obtain more comprehensive behavioral ratings for assessment and evaluation purposes and (2) provide more direct feedback to the client by allowing him to observe and/or hear his assertive responses. The client and counselor can use these tapes, stopping them at selected intervals for discussion or clarification. This process can expedite assertion training.

*Feedback and praise.* **Feedback** refers to the process whereby the client is given specific information about his performance. No judgmental attitudes or criticisms are used. Feedback should simply be objective and highly specific. For example, "You were not looking directly at Joan during that scene. You were either looking at the floor or the ceiling." Praise is often added to feedback when performance is good: "That was very good, John. You looked directly at Joan while you were talking to her. You're really doing well, today." Smiles, head nods, and other complimentary remarks also can serve to motivate the client to abide by instructions.

*Behavioral rehearsal.* Behavioral rehearsal is a fancy name for **practice**. Once the client is engaging in the appropriate responses, he must practice them over and over, via role playing. Continued practice will facilitate the transfer of these newly acquired assertive responses to the client's natural environment.

## Drink Refusal Training

A special case of assertiveness for alcoholics is the ability to refuse offers of alcoholic beverages by others. In fact, approximately one-third of alcoholic patients relapse as the direct result of social pressure from "friends." The ability to refuse drinks is much more difficult than it appears, but we often take this ability for granted when counseling alcoholics. The arguments used at social gatherings or by "drinking buddies" who stop by the house on Saturday evening are numerous: (1) "Oh come on, one drink won't hurt you," (2) "You must be awfully weak-willed if you can't handle one little drink," (3) "We're your friends. We won't let you have more than a couple," (4) "What's the matter, John, your wife won't let you drink?" (5) "Look, you've had a rough day. A couple of beers will help you relax," (6) "What kind of a friend are you?" (7) "What's the matter, do you think that you're better than everyone else?" (8) "John, you have to drink with these customers or you'll make them feel bad."

Dr. David Foy[4] has recently developed a specific method of teaching alcoholics how to refuse drinks effectively by using the technology of assertion training. Initially, at least three role-played scenes are constructed for each client, with each scene depicting a situation in which "friends" are enticing her to have a drink. The following scene is given as an example:

*Narrator*
You're at your brother's house. It's a special occasion and your whole family and several friends are there.

*Prompt from brother*
How about a beer?

Two counselors role play these scenes with the client, using many of the arguments listed above. Occasionally, alcohol will actually be available to more realistically simulate the natural environment. The client's responses are videotaped to assess her deficits.

Typically, the following components of an effective response are taught:

1. *Request a change:* Request the "pushers" to refrain from asking her to drink now or in the future.
2. *Offer an alternative:* Offer to engage in an activity that does not include drinking (e.g., "Why don't we go bowling this afternoon instead of drinking?").
3. *Change the subject:* Bring up new topics of conversation unrelated to drinking.
4. *Increase looking:* Look directly at the individual who is pressuring her when she makes her response.
5. *Use affects:* Speak in a loud voice and be serious when responding (i.e., not to smile or otherwise detract from sounding as though she really means what she is saying).

Each of these components is taught one at a time via focused instruction, modeling, behavioral rehearsal, and feedback. After a number of training sessions, the client is encouraged to try this new refusal response in her daily life. Usually, the client not only is able to refuse drinks more effectively but also experiences increased feelings of confidence and self-esteem over her own ability to modify one of the major precipitants of her problem drinking.

## Homework Assignments

After assertion training in the counselor's office is completed, the client must be given graded *homework assignments* to provide for the practice of assertiveness in the natural environment. Typically, the client and counselor select an interpersonal encounter that is likely to occur within the next week. Initially, this should be a situation that is relatively simple and straightforward and that will not result in severe anxiety for the client.

Fred and his counselor examine Fred's activities for the next week. He will be interacting with a number of people with whom, in the past, he has not expressed himself. For example, Fred's co-worker has been competing with Fred for an important position in the company and has been maliciously trying to cause trouble for Fred and make him look bad in front of his boss. Fred has been very angry about this situation, but instead of confronting his co-worker, he has been drinking heavily every evening. The counselor decides that this situation may be too emotionally charged for Fred to handle without some prior "assertive successes." Rather than deal with this major situation initially, Fred and his counselor agree on the following strategy: (1) during the following week, Fred will confront his secretary about her being late for work every day and request that she modify her behavior and (2) Fred will make a point to compliment his wife at least three times during the next week.

The counselor should, then, role play these situations with Fred a number of times to insure that he has a grasp of an effective response. When Fred returns for his next visit, the counselor should go over the specific details of exactly what happened in these situations. Fred's successes should be discussed, and he should be recognized for his efforts. Fred should also work on improvements in his assertiveness at this time, refining his responses. For example, he may have lacked the appropriate affect or eye contact when dealing with his secretary. The counselor should role play these scenes once again, requesting Fred to focus on those components which he found most difficult. Additional instructions and modeling may be needed at this time. It is very likely that Fred's initial attempts at assertiveness will be rewarded. That is, his secretary will probably be more punctual and his wife will probably reciprocate positive remarks. After these successes, Fred may be better prepared to handle his co-worker.

After a number of such successful experiences, clients usually will report that they are feeling much better about themselves. They will begin to feel more socially competent and more self-assured. These feelings should be discussed and reinforced by the counselor.

## THE CASE OF MILDRED: AN EXAMPLE

Having detailed the elements of training, we shall consider at length an example case of assertion training.

Mildred is a 38-year-old unmarried woman who lives with her invalid mother. She has been drinking heavily for 10 years, but she has been sober for the past month. In evaluating her behavior via a functional analysis, Mildred and her counselor begin to realize the relationships between Mildred's drinking binges and her lack of assertiveness. Her assertiveness is not general but is specific to her dealings with her mother and drinking friends. Based on Mildred's accounts of past episodes, she and the counselor role play the following scenes:

*Scene 1:* You are at home alone with your mother on a rainy Saturday afternoon. You feel bored and slightly depressed. Your friends stop by and want you to go out and have a few drinks.

| Role Model | Mildred |
|---|---|
| Come on Mildred, we'll have a good time. | Well, I don't know . . . . I really shouldn't. |
| Oh Mildred, a few drinks will cheer you up. | I'm not supposed to drink anymore. |
| Don't give me that. It's just a matter of time until you'll be drinking again, so you might as well start now. We're your friends. We'll take care of you. | Okay, but I'll just have *one* drink. |

*Scene 2:* You have spent the entire day cleaning the house while your mother was resting. You sit down and start reading a very enjoyable book. Your mother comes into the room and, in a very loud voice says:

| Role Model | Mildred |
|---|---|
| Mildred!! Look at you! Why don't you ever do anything around this house? You let your invalid mother do all of the housecleaning! | But mother, I *have* been trying to keep the house clean. |
| Look at that kitchen floor. It's filthy. | (No response.) |

*Scene 3:* You have just returned home from a shopping spree with a friend. You have been gone about two hours. Your mother says:

| Role Model | Mildred |
|---|---|
| Where have you been? You couldn't have been shopping this long. Let me smell your breath. I'll bet you've been drinking again! | Mother, I've just been shopping. You can smell my breath if you want to, but I haven't been drinking. |
| Don't lie to me. I can tell when you've been drinking. I knew you'd get started again. You're just no good, Mildred. What am I going to do with you. | (No response. Goes to her room.) |

All of Mildred's responses are very passive and compliant. She fails to look at the role model when delivering her response, she sounds very apologetic and unsure of herself, and she fails to ask the other person in these situations to modify her behavior. Using instructions and videotape feedback, Mildred learns to increase her eye contact, decrease her compliance, increase her assertive affect, and increase her requests for others to change their behavior. Mildred and her counselor practice these scenes more than 50 times during a number of counseling sessions.

Mildred's first homework assignment is to confront her drinking friends and to refuse to drink with them. In the next two weeks her friends come by and try to coax Mildred to have a drink with them. Mildred replies, "Look, you know that I've quit drinking and you know how miserable I am when I drink. If you were really my friends, you wouldn't try to get me to drink. I am not going to drink with you and please don't ask me ever again."

Mildred confessed to the counselor that she actually surprised herself with her own assertiveness. She did not think that she could do it. Her ability to confront her friends and deal with them effectively gave her a more positive feeling about herself and her future ability to refrain from alcohol.

With the encouragement and support of her counselor, Mildred began expressing her assertiveness toward her mother. She was able to firmly confront her mother about her unreasonable demands without becoming emotionally upset. Mildred noticed that although her mother did not seem to like her assertiveness (which she referred to as "impudence"), it was having an influence. Her mother became less demanding and easier to live with.

Mildred and her counselor also discussed the necessity for *positive* assertiveness toward her mother. Mildred had great difficulty in expressing positive feelings toward her mother even when the mother was behaving well. The counselor role played several positive remarks that Mildred could make to her mother with particular emphasis on affect and eye contact. Although Mildred was able to express these positive feelings toward her mother in the next several weeks, she had difficulty with eye contact. After a number of additional practice sessions, she improved on this component. Mildred reported that concomitantly her mother was returning her positive interactions and, despite occasional flareups, they were getting along well.

## IDENTIFYING WHEN AND WHERE TO BE ASSERTIVE
Once the client learns how to be assertive and begins trying out his new responses, he must learn the subtleties of assertiveness; i.e., when and where to use it. There is often a tendency on the part of novices to

overdo their newly acquired abilities. They do this by either over-responding when asserting themselves or being assertive in situations that do not require such behavior. Thus, the counselor must discuss each situation in which the client uses assertiveness in terms of the appropriateness and intensity of the response. There are situations which may require empathy and understanding rather than assertiveness. For example, if a friend who is distressed over personal problems or the death of a close relative reacts in a rude manner, it may be very inappropriate to be assertive to her. As mentioned earlier, when evaluating social situations in terms of assertiveness, the client must assess his response or potential response in terms of its:

1. *Effectiveness:* Will assertiveness accomplish my goal or change the situation?
2. *Effects on the target individual:* Is this individual so overly sensitive that my assertiveness might cause her undue emotional distress?
3. *Value from the client's standpoint:* Will this response enable me to feel better about the situation? Will this response settle the matter to the extent that I will not likely think about having a drink because of it?

## MAINTAINING ASSERTIVENESS

The long-term maintenance of assertiveness appears related to three factors: (1) periodic follow-up counseling sessions, (2) continued use of assertiveness by the client, and (3) response of others to the client's assertiveness.

Follow-up contacts with the client are essential to maintain not only assertive behaviors but also other alternative behavioral skills acquired in counseling. During the sessions, assertive situations can be discussed and the client's responses assessed. Role playing during these sessions is necessary to help the client to further refine his assertiveness and also to insure that the client has maintained his skills. The counselor should always remember that the client may be providing positive follow-up information either to please the counselor or to avoid confrontation.

These follow-up sessions encourage the client to use assertiveness. As with any skill, the more frequently it is used, the more adept the client will become in its use. Once the client becomes lax in its use, he may find it more difficult to behave assertively when necessary.

The reactions of others to the client's assertiveness are also very important. Both the counselor and client must remember that friends and relatives have learned to deal with the client on a basis of certain expectations. Since persons function in behavioral-interactional *systems,* when one component of the system changes, other components must readjust. Even though friends and relatives may be pleased with the client's new coping methods, their initial reactions may include bewilderment, confusion, and even hostility. They often are not certain whether these changes will last and, on the basis of the client's past failures at behavior change, they often are pessimistic. The counselor must discuss these reactions with these close friends or relatives of the client. They must be prepared to verbally reward the client for his assertiveness. In many instances, other members of the family must also receive assertion training to help them better cope with problems on an equal plane with the client.

Of course, the client will experience failures with his assertiveness. Occasionally assertiveness will not work or may result in verbal abuse from the target. The client will be able to deal with these instances if he has enough other experiences with assertive successes. It is often the counselor's responsibility to program these successes through family counseling or counseling with the client's friends.

## Footnotes

1. J. Wolpe and A. Lazarus. *Behavior therapy techniques.* New York: Pergamon Press, Inc., 1966.

2. S. A. Rathus. A 30-item schedule for assessing assertive behavior. *Behavior Therapy,* 1973, *4,* 398-406.

3. R. M. Eisler, P. M. Miller, and M. Hersen. Components of assertive behavior. *Journal of Clinical Psychology* 1973, *29,* 295-299.

4. D. W. Foy, P. M. Miller, R. M. Eisler, and D. H. O'Toole. Social skills training to teach alcoholics to refuse drinks effectively. *Journal of Alcohol Studies,* 1976, *37,* 1340-1345.

# 6 Social and Marital Skills Training

*PROBLEMS OF ALCOHOLICS*

Statistics show that alcoholics have a higher divorce rate and a greater number of marriages per person than nonalcoholics, are involved in more antisocial behavior, and have a higher incidence of violence in the family.[1] Most workers would agree that the majority of problem drinkers are deficient in social and marital skills. The importance of this factor is evidenced by the vast number of alcoholism rehabilitation programs which include the remediation of interpersonal problems.

The approach that counseling takes varies according to the theoretical framework and training of the alcoholism counselor. These approaches include (1) individual and group therapy based on client-centered counseling techniques, (2) milieu therapy in which the client is given the experience of positive interactions with staff members as well as with other clients, (3) the direct approach based on confronting clients with their maladaptive behaviors, and the (4) behavioral approach in which the principles of reinforcement, punishment, extinction, and shaping are used. The effectiveness of any of these approaches depends on the skill of the counselor and the importance of the therapeutic goals to the client. In this chapter, we will discuss assessment of the social and marital skills available to the alcoholic client and training techniques for skills in areas found deficient.

Although the division is artificial, we will discuss social skills apart from marital skills, intending, however, for the counselor to use what is appropriate in both sections for each client.

Each of us has certain interactional behaviors on which we rely to get what we want from others and to live in relative harmony. A child's repertoire is limited and mostly based on negative reinforcement. For example, crying ceases when the child gets what she desires. The child cries loudly until Father picks her up, thus reinforcing Father for this action and in return being reinforced for crying. As the child matures, she learns other ways of getting what she wants. By the time she reaches young adulthood her repertoire includes effective and subtle skills as well as those which were used in the first attempts at behavior modification of significant others.

An adult must have a full array of techniques available to her to interact successfully with others. Included in these techniques are the sending of readable verbal and nonverbal cues and the accurate reading of such cues sent from others. Together, these techniques compose the individual's style of communication.

Gorad, McCourt, and Cobb maintain that there is a style of communication shared by all alcoholics, regardless of personality type or the presence of intoxication.[2] These researchers describe the primary feature of this style as the avoidance of responsibility for communication. Ambiguous statements, passive posturing, method of articulation, especially when intoxicated, choice of words, and the discrepancy between the verbal and nonverbal message are thought to exemplify the alcoholic style.

Whether one agrees completely with these authors or not, the alcoholic person *does* seem to draw on a limited range of interactional behavior and elicits just as limited a range of reactions. These inevitably include frustration, sympathy, anger, and feelings of being manipulated by the alcoholic. With little positive feedback from others, the alcoholic may withdraw, becoming a social isolate and turning to alcohol to relieve boredom and frustration.

Too, drinking may relieve inhibitions and assist the person in coping with and even enjoying social situations. One would have to offer an extremely attractive alternative to counter the reinforcing value of the alcohol.

Social and marital skills training may be this alternative. Teaching the client more adaptive ways to get what he wants, to develop relationships, and to feel comfortable socially lessens the need for alcohol in these situations. Thus, a plan for therapeutic intervention is developed. It is based on analysis of the *antecedents, consequences,* and *maintaining factors* associated with the social and marital problem.

## ASSESSMENT

Although we have previously covered the basic techniques of assessment, we will review them and mention some points especially pertinent to social- and marital-skills counseling. The data on which assessment is based may be collected in several ways. *Self-report* is the most widely used method. Here, we rely on the client's description of the problem. Self-report is valuable in that the emotional content of the situation as well as the client's perception of it is available. Its drawbacks include selectivity of report and misperception of events. These handicaps are lessened when validating information is obtained from an observer or another participant. For example, a man may have perceived that his wife misunderstood his remark about her job and so drank heavily that evening. The wife may have reported a vague feeling of depression which seemed unconnected to any preceding events. Valuable information was gained by the cooperation of the spouse.

*Direct observation* of the client's behavior gives the counselor information not readily available under other conditions. This is especially true of nonverbal behavior, such as posture, tone of voice, and facial expression. Ideally, observation is carried out in the client's natural environment or under the controlled conditions of the laboratory. Unfortunately, such conditions are unavailable to most counselors. Effective use of direct observation can be carried out in the counselor's office, however. If the client and spouse are being seen jointly, much information can be gleaned by allowing the couple some leeway in their interaction. The counselor can determine the interactional style of the couple, the manner in which each controls the other, and the strengths and weaknesses of the unit.

A more structured use of direct observation consists of the client picturing himself in a situation described by the counselor and acting out his role as he would in real life. A wealth of information may be obtained in this way and may be used in individual, couple, family, or group therapy. For example, Judy expressed ambivalent feelings about her long-term relationship with Marty. She wanted the option of other relationships; yet when Marty agreed to this, she argued that he had lost interest in her and wanted to end their friendship. She threatened to leave him first, interrupted his protests, stomped back and forth the length of the room, and refused to lower her voice. Finally, frustrated, Marty left. Judy, feeling remorseful, comforted herself with alcohol. This was the pattern of behavior which became more clear when she and her counselor acted it out during a session. Judy could see the double bind she had used on Marty and the need to learn more appropriate ways of expressing her fears of desertion. By having the client act out the situation, the counselor could observe the affect and mixed messages that Judy used. Thus, counseling would include teaching Judy to take responsibility for expressing accurately her thoughts and feelings.

A third method of assessment is the use of *scales and inventories* such as the Marital Happiness Scale (Azrin, Naster, and Jones, 1973; see Table 5 in Chapter 2). These tests rely on the client's thoughts or feelings about a situation. They are useful because their simplicity makes them feasible to use at certain checkpoints throughout therapy. They also are useful as reports for the clients to discuss.

## ELEMENTS OF TRAINING

Training is based on a program of *information, modeling* (demonstrating the proper behavior), *behavioral rehearsal* (allowing the client to practice the particular behavior), *feedback* (telling the client what was good and what needs improvement), *home assignments,* and *praise.* Information may include the social expectations particular to the individual's age, sex, and marital status. Demonstration, practice, and feedback may be conducted in individual sessions or in groups. There are many advantages to teaching social skills in groups. They include the greater opportunity for feedback and social praise and the availability of both sexes for practice.

## SOCIAL-SKILLS TRAINING

As sexual roles and social expectations change, the need to develop a flexible set of social skills becomes important. This is especially true of the lone problem drinker or of the client whose social circle may be composed solely of drinking partners. One aspect of a treatment program must be the development of a pleasure system that is not based on drinking. This is especially necessary because drinking partners tend to press the abstaining drinker into taking "just one" by prodding or embarrassing him. Clients usually recognize the need to restructure their social life, but they may become easily frustrated in the attempt. Disassociating oneself from drinking buddies can cause loneliness, which is just as dangerous to the client's treatment as his being with the heavy drinkers. The counselor will find clients in need of a great deal of support during this time. They usually are in need also of specific social-skills training.

According to the results of assessment, attention may focus on certain of the following areas: how to initiate social contacts, how to develop friendships, what expectations are realistic, where to go for leisure.

### Initiating Social Contacts

The counselor and the client will find it necessary to determine safe areas *where* the probability of meeting people in nonalcohol-related situations is high. It has almost become traditional to include in this category such places as libraries, parks, laundromats, special interest clubs, and work. In developing safe areas for an individual, the following guidelines are helpful:

1. The place should not have alcohol as a major focal point.
2. There should be others present who are likely to be receptive to meeting new people.
3. It should be accepted that one may engage another in conversation.
4. Some places are more acceptable by the above guidelines; others require greater skill for success.

*When* to approach someone plays a large part in success of the encounter. It is unwise to expect the client will be rewarded when approaching someone deep in conversation with a companion. Here, too, guidelines may help the client. Contact can be initiated:

1. When the client is in a place on the list of appropriate areas.
2. When the person or people *look* approachable. (For example, she is alone, smiles, is looking around the area).
3. When the client *feels* confident enough to approach.

*How* to initiate social contacts is probably the area which will require the greatest cooperative work between the counselor and the client. Not only the development of skills but also the lessening of anxiety associated with initiating social contact will be necessary.

The initial social contact differs in some respects from later interactions. The individual must rely on appearance and nonverbal communication to a greater extent in the first contact. She must risk failure or rebuke or other negative experiences. However, the client must be made to realize that the alternative is the loss of opportunities to make a friendship.

In this area there seems to be several issues of importance in how one approaches another. Discrete behaviors such as talking, looking, and being in close contact can be identified. Timing also is important. Proficiency comes with practice. Table 7 may be used as a reference in teaching the client how to make initial contact.

One or two skills are taught each session. It is essential that the client practice outside the counseling session. A client may be able to verbalize correct social skills, but because of anxiety, he may be unable to use them when the opportunity presents itself.

## Case Study Of Social-Skills Training

A typical situation is one in which a recently divorced male client became anxious whenever he talked with a woman whom he suspected would like to go out with him. He became anxious and would lose

## TABLE 7. STEPS IN INITIATING SOCIAL CONTACT

*Evaluation of the situation:* Situations which the client is most likely to encounter are evaluated for effectiveness. Such situations include approaching a male, a female, a stranger, a group of same sex, and a group of both sexes.

*Selection procedure:* Using guidelines in earlier sections will help the client to select the appropriate person, place, and procedure.

*Introductory statement:* *Verbal*—Certain stock phrases may be necessary for the client to use ("Hello, I'm Bill Green. I see you have the Sunday Times. Are you from New York?"; "May I join you? I'm Jane Smith"; at a party buffet line, "The food looks delicious. Have you tried any yet?").
*Nonverbal*—A smile and eye contact are as important as verbal contact.

*Conversation flow:* *Verbal*—Listening, feedback, questioning (discussed in a later section) are good skills for the beginning conversationalist to develop in that they give a greater balance to the burden of conversational flow. For handling silences, the client should have some topics available for discussion.
*Nonverbal*—Expressions of interest and pauses are examples.

*Termination:* *Verbal*—Stock phrases are useful ("I have to go now"). The client need not feel compelled to elaborate on reasons for termination.
*Nonverbal*—Picking up cues from the participants that they wish to end the conversation is especially important.

*Follow-up:* The counselor and client should discuss ways to develop the relationship into friendship (e.g., "May I see you again?"). Appropriateness of the steps in the relationship should be stressed.

*Other:* How to handle rebuke, how to develop good timing, evaluating performance, levels of involvement, and setting limits should be stressed in training.

track of his thoughts. Although he would have liked the friendship to develop, he began avoiding her. In discussing the problem with his counselor, the client found that his fears concerned his inability to believe a woman might find him attractive, his reluctance to risk hurt so soon after his divorce, and his need to update his social skills.

A treatment plan devised by the counselor was based on supportive counseling in which the client was encouraged to discuss his divorce, his beginning adjustment as a single person, and his fears of being hurt in relationships. He was also given relaxation training (discussed in Chapter 4) in preparation for a program to update his social skills. Limited training and small tasks were assigned until the client felt ready to work directly on his presenting problem. In taking into account the anxieties of the client, the counselor probably made longer-lasting progress.

### Expectations And Involvement Levels

A word should be said about the setting of limits and the levels of involvement. *It is a common mistake of those just learning social skills to expect total involvement from those with whom they become acquainted.* This is an immature reaction and the one expectation that frequently frightens others away. The counselor may combat part of this expectation simply by discussing with the client the levels of involvement and what each level entails. Seeking instant intimacy during the acquaintance stage will cause negative reactions from others. A rule of thumb for beginners is that it is better to go a bit more slowly than to have to back up because of misunderstandings. In addition to this is the setting of limits for oneself and for the new acquaintance or friend. By limits we mean amount of time, emotional investment, and types of activities and investment needed to meet expectations. The counselor will most likely have to devote at least one session to these two areas: expectations and limits.

### MARITAL-SKILLS TRAINING

People marry because they expect in that way to have certain pleasures more available to them. Anticipated pleasures for married individuals may include companionship, children, security, sex, and social acceptance. There also are responsibilities and annoyances specific to the married state. Although less attention usually is given to them before marriage, they too shape the relationship. Among them are household and child-care duties, restructuring of time, and the need to compromise in sexual, financial, and goal-setting areas in general.

## Improving Communication

Most couples verbalize as primary concern a lack of communication. They often can see their pattern of ignoring one another, anticipating negative replies, interrupting or screaming at one another, and even resorting to physical assault. Teaching the two how to communicate in an open, nonthreatening manner provides the basis for work in other areas. Unless they can state their wishes and concerns, no long-lasting positive effect can occur in financial, sexual, or social areas. The excerpt from a session with Joan and Harry illustrates this:

| Joan | Harry |
|---|---|
| I want to go home for the holidays to see my folks. | Your family always comes first. You can never think of me and what I want. |
| How can you say that! Didn't I leave Chicago to come here with you? You are a selfish, immature, . . . . | Wait a minute! Who do you think you are, calling me names? I have a good mind to . . . . |
| To what? If it weren't for your drinking . . . . | |

If someone asked this couple what the opening statement had been, they probably could not reply because they would have forgotten. This excerpt shows communication faults typical of many couples who are seen in therapy. They each *assumed* they knew how the other was feeling or what the other was thinking ("Your family always comes first"). They *name-called* ("selfish, immature"). They *interrupted* ("Wait a minute!"). They brought in other people and other subjects ("your family"; "your drinking"). We can assume their voices were raised and they were aggressive in nonverbal ways as well.

These persons may be adept and considerate of others in social settings, but in relating to one another, they become careless in the use of basic skills of communication. Brownstone and Dye have used structured sessions to teach the skills of speaking and listening.[3] In these sessions participants are allowed to practice the components of good communication on neutral topics. As the skills are learned, the participants discuss more troublesome topics. Table 8 is an adaptation of Brownstone and Dye's guidelines.

Part of marital counseling in communications is teaching the couple how to argue and disagree. Some like to describe this as teaching the rules of fair fighting. Unchecked negative interactions can be

## TABLE 8. COMMUNICATION GUIDELINES

*Speaker*

1. Be specific. Example (right): "I would like to discuss next month's vacation plans."

2. Attend to own voice and non-verbal cues. Example (wrong): (Loudly and frowning) "No, I'm not angry!"

3. Don't nag or be repetitive; be courteous. Example (right): "Excuse me now, but I'm still on the phone."

4. Don't monopolize the conversation.

5. Don't put another on defense by name calling, accusing, or insinuating. Example (wrong): "You certainly were friendly with Joe at the party tonight."

6. Check to be sure the listener understands what you are saying. Example (right): "Did I make myself clear?"

7. Be honest and direct in stating your ideas, feelings, or wishes, but do not present them in such a way that the other person feels impelled to agree. Example (wrong): "I'm sure you want to go to that movie, too."

8. Focus on giving and getting information to solve a problem. Example (right): "I had planned to drive to the grocery store. What time did you expect to leave here?"

*Listener*

1. Listen actively by
   a. giving the speaker your full attention.
   b. looking at the speaker.
   c. asking questions as a check to understanding; paraphrasing.
   d. avoiding interrupting.
   e. waiting until the speaker is finished before responding.

2. Be open-minded to new information the speaker may have.

3. Avoid getting angry because the speaker holds a different viewpoint.

4. Find out why the speaker holds a certain viewpoint.

5. Show a sympathetic attitude by recognizing the speaker's feelings and concerns.

6. Check that everyone involved is clear on decisions which are made.

destructive to the marital relationship. Most couples argue in a manner that leaves partners necessarily defensive and vulnerable at their most sensitive points. Bad feelings between the two and a reluctance to interact in any but safe areas are by-products of most arguments. These by-products are eliminated when certain rules or steps are followed (see Table 9).

---

*TABLE 9. RULES FOR NEGATIVE INTERACTIONS*

1. Rather than wait for a problem to escalate, discuss it as soon as it becomes apparent.
2. However, postpone the argument until each partner is calm enough to discuss the problem.
3. Choose a private place and a time when neither person will be interrupted.
4. The complaintant should state fully the problem as she/he sees it.
5. The partner should listen without verbal or nonverbal comment until the complaintant has finished.
6. The partner may now ask for clarification, add new information, apologize, deny, or discuss solutions—whichever is appropriate.
7. Before deciding on a solution, each should have a chance to relate the emotional impact the discussion is having.
8. Neither should:
   a. bring in past events or other people
   b. berate, call names, become controlling by crying, frowning, etc.
   c. attack by bringing in sensitive material not pertinent to the argument
   d. leave the discussion without at least a tentative solution
   e. concede or give in simply to stop the discussion or for secondary gains

---

Communications-skills training may be used with individuals, couples, or small groups. The counselor acts as teacher, arbitrator, and demonstrator. This is a slow process better done in stepwise fashion over several sessions and with home practice assigned between sessions. The use of audiotapes and videotapes is helpful in giving the couple feedback.

## Teaching Reciprocal Interactions

Dr. Richard Stuart suggests that good marital relationships are based on the balance of giving and obtaining reinforcers.[4] The marital partners will need to re-evaluate their effectiveness from time to time. Marriage is seen as a fluid relationship changing over time as the needs of the partners change. Many couples realize the marital contract is an evolving one only as they outgrow the original conditions. Many may feel disappointed and angry. For the couple who also must deal with the problem of alcohol, the letdown is even more difficult to handle. When counseling is finally sought, the couple must face the realization that the marriage has indeed evolved. Before, they may have shared concerns, spent leisure time together, and planned future goals; now they lead quite separate lives, with their interaction based largely on arguments and bickering over drinking or finances or the discipline of their children. Positive interactions are only minimal at this point.

**Reciprocity counseling** teaches a couple how to maximize the number and kind of positive interactions. The system is based on the giving of reinforcers only when the partner is also giving pleasure. In evaluating their present relationship, areas in which pleasure is currently being given are uncovered. This is an important preliminary step in that it encourages the two to make the emotional investment necessary to improve their relationship. Generally, marital complaints may be attributed to certain of the following areas: there are too few pleasures; the pleasures are derived from a limited area of interactions, such as financial; pleasure given is not adequately reciprocated; the partner giving the pleasure is not acknowledged; certain pleasures may have lost their intensity for satisfying; certain other pleasures may be newly desired, but not forthcoming; communication concerning adequacy of pleasures in particular areas may be faulty; marital demands may impose on nonmarital pleasure sources; the couple may be using punishment, such as nagging or ignoring, to obtain what they desire.

On the basis of the above analysis, the goal of counseling will be to establish reciprocal reinforcement by teaching the couple how to gain more pleasure from each area. They are encouraged to keep records of their goals and of times pleasures are given so that the effectiveness of intervention can be assessed. Since couples naturally interact and should give and receive reinforcers simultaneously in many areas, counseling, too, may seek to develop pleasure in several areas simultaneously. The alternative to this approach is to work on two or three areas initially, adding others as counseling progresses. Examples of both approaches follow:

A. *The multi-area approach:* The couple chooses one or two goals for each area.
   1. *Household responsibilities:* Specific duties such as cleaning, meal preparation, laundry.
   2. *Rearing of children:* Discipline, physical care, babysitting, entertainment.
   3. *Financial:* Bill paying; decisions on spending, savings, and personal allowances.
   4. *Social:*
      a. *With each other:* Setting engagements, inviting others to share time, spending time alone away from home, using alcohol.
      b. *Independently:* Deciding on amount of independent social time, planning for overlap of independent time, babysitters, car use, money spending.
   5. *Sexual:* Frequency, time, affection other than intercourse, jealousy.
   6. *Career:* Amount of time spent in its pursuit, education; impact on family of dual-career couples.
   7. *Communication:* Planned discussion times, use of problem solving, arguments, misunderstandings.
   8. *Long-range goal setting:* Discussion of goal setting and planning, setting of priorities.
B. *Limited-area approach:* The counselor helps the couple choose one or two areas in which to work.
   1. *Household duties:* Care of the house, care of the grounds.
   2. *Social:* Handling independent activities, arranging engagement in advance so planning is not hurried, sharing use of the car.
   3. *Communication:* Developing problem-solving skills, learning to clarify points.

Each approach has advantages and disadvantages that the counselor should consider when beginning work with a couple. The multi-area approach is more like real life in that various pleasures are given simultaneously rather than in area blocks. However, in the multi-area approach, people trying to develop pleasure in a specific area may rely on more easily given pleasures, which may slow development of weaker areas. The opposite is true of the second approach. Since attention is focused on a limited area, more practice is given so development may be quicker. However, incorporation of skills into everyday life becomes an additional step. The extent of marital discord, the couple's interest, and their grasp of the concept of reciprocal reinforcement are some considerations in deciding which approach to use.

A contract outlining the pleasure desired in each area may be developed at this point. (Behavioral contracts are discussed more fully later in this chapter.)

In the counseling sessions the partners are taught to give reinforcement when they get pleasure and to withhold it until they obtain pleasure themselves. They are given practice in feedback technique and in asking for feedback. (This is more fully discussed later in the chapter.) For example, Joe stated that even though he had a difficult day, he didn't stop at the bar after work. In the past, his wife would sympathize with him on his difficult day, criticizing his boss and fellow workers but would ignore his accomplishment. During a counseling session Joe told his wife what impact her comments had and requested she compliment him on his self-control. Joe gave his wife feedback which then could be used to alter her own feedback to him.

As counseling progresses, positive interactions increase. Couples begin to spend more time together so that the possibility that pleasures will occur also increases. Additionally, others are drawn to the couple now that there is less tension between them; therefore, the range of pleasure is continually increasing.

The same procedures of demonstration, practice, feedback, and home practice are used here as were outlined in the other skill areas.

## Reasons For Poor Interaction

As we mentioned previously, a couple may have and use good social skills with strangers and friends but have minimal positive interaction with each other. Several factors may be relevant. As people become more familiar, they become less concerned with "appearances." They may become lazy, finding it easier to give a quick command than to make a request. Also, with more time spent together and with the sharing of everyday problems, the marital partner becomes a safe and convenient target of one's anger and frustration. Unable to tell the boss that a directive is unfair, a person lets tension mount until a safe target is found. The chance that a spouse will tolerate displaced hostility is greater than the chance that a friend or stranger will. Knowing this, couples frequently find themselves taking advantage of the situation. A study by Birchler, Weiss, and Vincent showed this to be so.[5] Distressed couples used less punishing and more pleasurable interactional patterns with strangers. The exact opposite was true for their own interaction; that is, more aversive and less positive behaviors occurred.

## Developing Positive Problem-Solving Behaviors

Using a Marital Interaction Coding System, the authors defined positive (facilitative) and negative (nonfacilitative) problem-solving behaviors in the following way. **Positive statements** included the offering of a solution to the problem, acceptance of responsibility for the solution to the problem, and willingness to compromise. **Negative statements** which were seen in nonfacilitative problem solving included complaining, criticizing, denying responsibility, making excuses, directing put-downs to the spouse, interrupting, and disagreeing.

The following case study will demonstrate the development of positive or facilitative problem solving. Subsequent to the teaching of problem solving, the counselor and the couple independently describe how they solve a problem. Their report follows:

*Wife*

We usually *ignore the problem* until it is simply too big to ignore any longer. Then he comes *screaming*, holding a bill or something and shakes it at me. I've learned to *walk away*; otherwise, his screaming goes on and on. Finally, *he'll calm down* and pay the bill. There's *no communication* between us *for several days*. Then something, I don't know what, gets us talking again.

*Husband*

*I expect* her to pay the bills but *she just can't take responsibility for anything.* Finally, *I'll have to* do the work. When I *ask her about it,* she *looks at me in a contemptuous way* and walks away. That infuriates me even more and if I follow her I know we'd be throwing things before long so I just *go back to paying the bills. It's not too pleasant* around the house after that.

The reports will be the basis for a remedial program in problem solving. The counselor and couple together have underlined the major areas of difficulty. The categories are:

1. lack of workable system of handling bills
2. putting of responsibility on the other mate
3. reacting to the individual problem rather than developing a usable solution
4. carry-over to other parts of their life together

The couple will be encouraged to offer several solutions for discussion before accepting one. In this example, they might include:

1. setting a monthly or weekly time to pay all bills
2. jointly meeting on a regular basis to pay bills

3. alternating bill-paying responsibilities monthly
4. making each responsible for half the bills

The couple are encouraged to brainstorm so that all possible solutions are listed. Each is considered in turn. If one cannot be decided on, the couple must compromise. It is important that they understand that one may have to concede more than the other. At times this is unavoidable, but one partner should not be placed in this role continually.

The couple are then asked to try the plan for a stated period of time. At the end of that time, adjustments may be made.

Although the counseling session is devoted to a specific problem, the problem-solving procedure is similar for all problems. The goal here is to teach the skills of problem solving so that the couple can work out solutions independently of the counselor.

## USING INTERPERSONAL SKILLS EFFECTIVELY

Research is being reported which suggests that a person may have adequate or good interpersonal skills but be unable to use them effectively. Researchers have found that some persons misjudged their adequacy; others were skillful only in certain areas; still others were found to be hindered by the anxiety they experienced in social situations.

Therefore, one aspect of social- and marital-skills training is the effective use of skills learned or developed in counseling. Anxiety must be relieved when it causes persons to avoid social situations or makes them unable to use the interpersonal skills which they do have. This can be accomplished by using relaxation training (discussed in Chapter 4) and by setting small goals which the individual can achieve without the interfering anxiety. The systematic setting of more difficult goals based on the achievement of the easier ones will reinforce the client's use of skills and assure her entering social situations. An example of this is the case of Carl, an alcoholic. Although drinking had not been a problem for him in quite some time, he feared going to parties where alcohol would be served, because he thought someone might persist in offering him drinks until he would give in. Consequently, his social life was so curtailed that he and his wife spent most of their free time together. His wife was becoming more intolerant of the situation and had decided she would go to the next party alone.

The counselor suggested Carl begin relaxation training. In addition, they practiced ways to handle the situation. These ways included refusing without offering a reason, stating he had just finished a drink, refusing and offering a medical excuse, refusing and asking the person next to him a question or immediately walking away.

The counselor also suggested Carl and his wife invite several people to their home where they would be in the position of offering drinks rather than having drinks offered to them. Once Carl became comfortable in that situation, he went to a friend's party, first informing the friend of his wish to abstain. He also set time limits, staying only an hour and lengthening that time as parties became easier for him to handle. His wife also was used as a cohort in sharing the responsibility of lessening an anxious situation. Slowly and in a cooperative manner, Carl and his wife were able to achieve their goal.

There are times when an individual is in a poor position to evaluate her handling of a situation. Asking others for feedback is most useful at this time. The counselor, a good friend, a spouse, or family member might serve in this capacity. The example of two friends, Jane and Marsha, will illustrate this. Jane and Marsha were both invited for coffee by a co-worker. Marsha declined, saying she had a report to finish. Jane, frowning at Marsha, said she'd be happy to go. Later, when the two were together Marsha brought up the incident:

| *Marsha* | *Jane* |
|---|---|
| Jane, why didn't you make an excuse not to go for coffee? | How did you know I didn't want to go? I thought I was being most pleasant. |
| You were, except for the frown you gave me. | |

That bit of information helped Jane see that she needed more practice in refusing invitations. She also understood why her co-worker became distant.

*The request for feedback* can also serve as a source for immediate praise or correction. It helps an individual to learn how "to read" the listener. The client can use such statements as "Am I making my point clear?" "What is your reaction?" "What do you think about that?" "What are your feelings?"

The client also gives feedback, stating whether she agrees or disagrees with the speaker, and why. Feedback is a quick and convenient way to reinforce another and obtain reinforcement.

Nonverbal feedback, such as smiling, frowning, nodding, and turning away, is given even more freely and more universally. The client who learns to send and receive nonverbal feedback accurately is in a good position to evaluate and readjust her behavior.

Long-term friends and partners are quite adept at reading one another while others may miss the interaction completely. In difficult or new situations, prearranged nonverbal signals between the client and a friend or spouse may serve as guidelines. A raised eyebrow informs the receiver that she is entering upon an unsafe topic.

The individual with a drinking problem may use both verbal and nonverbal feedback to dissuade the speaker from a discourse on alcoholism or some other touchy subject. "I would rather not discuss it" can be effective when said in a neutral voice tone. A quick reply and an immediate change of subject is also a good way to handle this.

As one uses social skills, there will be opportunity to refine technique, adjusting the use of certain approaches and discarding others. As with most behaviors, the ability to interact with people in a pleasant, reinforcing manner is an evolving one, continually in need of maintenance and improvement. New situations, new people, and new expanding roles for all adults will call for more flexible interpersonal skills.

## CONTRACTS IN SOCIAL- AND MARITAL-SKILLS TRAINING

Behavioral contracts can help clients develop social and marital skills. Form 2 is an example of a behavioral contract which was composed with the assistance of the client's counselor. It states precisely what must occur for the participants to obtain pleasure. The contract is *negotiated* until it meets with the approval of all participants. In this way, clients are held responsible for carrying out the agreement they signed, and misunderstandings are eliminated. Compromise is a necessary condition of contracts.

Behavioral contracts may be negotiated between the client and the spouse, family members, or other significant persons, such as the client's friends. It is desirable to have members of the client's community, rather than just the counselor, participate. Although a contract may be negotiated between the counselor and client so that the number of sessions, for example, is decided upon at the onset, typically the counselor acts as consultant and teacher.

Contracting may be used in a wide range of situations including the development of *deficient behaviors,* such as the display of affection toward marital partners; the reduction of excessive behaviors, such as screaming and shouting when angry; the increase of positive behaviors, such as initiating conversation with new acquaintances.

The following steps are taken in the development of a behavioral contract:

1. Participants independently list behavior changes desired. The behaviors should be as specific as possible (see Table 10).

2. The counselor assists the participants in choosing *target behaviors*. These behaviors, taken from the list in Step 1, are those on which the participants agree to work. One to three behaviors are an optimal number on which to work.
3. The participants, with the counselor's assistance, *negotiate* the *consequences* of the target behaviors. Contracts are best built on reinforcement which each participant previously listed as positive for him or her (see Table 11).
4. A time limit is appropriate with many contracts. At the termination date, the contract may be extended or re-negotiated by the participants.

It is necessary that participants record initial *base rates* of the behaviors to be changed so that the effectiveness of the contract can be evaluated. To obtain the base rate, each participant counts the number of times the listed behaviors are elicited by the other participants. It is helpful to use a recording form rather than to expect the participants to rely on memory (see Form 3).

---

*FORM 2.   BEHAVIORAL CONTRACT*

Name of participants:  _____

Date of agreement:  _____

We agree to the following:

A.   Client X will not visit Joe's Tavern for the next month if, in return, Friend Y agrees to invite him to her home one evening each weekend for the next month.

B.   Friend Y will invite Client X to her home one evening each weekend if, in return, Client X refrains from visiting Joe's Tavern the previous week days.

Client   _____

Friend   _____

Witness   _____

---

FORM 3.   SHEET FOR RECORDING
          INITIAL BASE RATE OF BEHAVIORS

Data Record

Target Behaviors defined:  1.
                           2.
                           3.

| Date | Time | Behavior | Place | Outcome |
|------|------|----------|-------|---------|
|      |      |          |       |         |
|      |      |          |       |         |
|      |      |          |       |         |
|      |      |          |       |         |
|      |      |          |       |         |

TABLE 10.   CLIENT'S LIST
            OF DESIRED BEHAVIOR CHANGES

1. To have George spend less time at work and more with me
   (specific).
2. To stop being depressed (nonspecific). The counselor should assist
   the client in determining the *antecedents* of the depression as well
   as other important points.
3. To have June remain sober at parties (specific).
4. To have the children share in certain household duties (specific).

| TABLE 11. | POSITIVE REINFORCERS (PLEASURES) AS CONSEQUENCES |
|---|---|

1. Spending time alone
2. Spending time with another
3. Going to a restaurant
4. Going to a movie
5. Receiving compliments
6. Receiving material gift/clothing
7. Watching a specific TV show
8. Visiting a friend

## Footnotes

1. N. Azrin, B. Naster, and R. Jones. Reciprocity counseling: A rapid learning-based procedure for marital counseling. *Behaviour Research and Therapy,* 1973, *11,* 365-382.

2. S. L. Gorad, W. F. McCourt, and J. C. Cobb. A communication approach to alcoholism. *Quarterly Journal of Studies on Alcohol,* 1971, *32,* 651-668.

3. J. Brownstone and C. Dye. *Communication workshop for parents of adolescents.* Champaign, IL: Research Press, 1973.

4. R. Stuart. Operant-interpersonal treatment for marital discord. *Journal of Consulting and Clinical Psychology,* 1969, *33,* 675-682.

5. G. R. Birchler, R. L. Weiss, and J. P. Vincent. Multimethod analysis of social reinforcement exchange between maritally distressed and nondistressed spouse and stranger dyads. *Journal of Personality and Social Psychology,* 1975, *31*(2), 349-360.

# 7 Sex Counseling

## GROWING INTEREST IN SEXUALITY

Until recently the client's sexual problems were ignored or at best simply acknowledged by the counselor. There were many reasons for this including lack of knowledge concerning human sexuality, discomfort associated with discussion of sexuality, and denial of the importance of sexuality in our lives. There is still much misunderstanding, misinformation, and discomfort surrounding this aspect of our lives; however, a new atmosphere of interest has developed. Men and women want to know why they respond sexually, how they can realize themselves as sexual as well as intellectual and moral beings, and what they can do if they experience sexual difficulty.

The past 10 years has seen a new openness and interest in "personal" sexuality, as opposed to faceless, immature, "object" sexuality. Although the work of many writers has formed the basis for development, Masters and Johnson and Albert Ellis may be credited with publicizing and making legitimate the research of human sexuality and the treatment of sexual problems.

The need for sensitive, qualified, and effective sex counseling has led to sex manuals being placed on the best seller list and the development of sex clinics throughout the United States. Counselors have come to realize that sexual problems must be dealt with as part of their usual work. Clients with some complicated sexual problems should be referred to trained sex therapists.

## ALCOHOL AND SEXUALITY

It should be noted that men and women with alcohol problems usually suffer some form of sexual dysfunction. The alcoholic suffers the effects of alcohol on his (or her) sexuality in several ways. First, sexual promiscuity may occur more readily.[1] Second, the alcoholic may suffer an inability to perform sexually because of the physiologically depressing effects of alcohol. Researchers believe that because of alcohol abuse some males may suffer irreversible damage on the neurogenic reflex arc serving the process of erection.[2] Third, the interpersonal relationship upon which a good sexual relationship is based may become so distorted because of the problems of the alcoholic and her partner that the sexual relationship is impossible to maintain.

The effect of sexual difficulty on the alcoholic client is a severe blow when coupled, as it is, with other problems. The client must be made to understand that the sexual response is as sensitive to disruption as any other response and that a treatment plan in which sexual difficulties are handled along with other problems is needed.

Always, the techniques we outline are offered to develop a personal sexuality based on a full interpersonal relationship. We make no assumptions about the best kind of partners or relationships so long as there is a base of understanding, love, and kindness between the partners. We see the sexual relationship as another aspect of the broader interpersonal one for which we all strive. We use technique only to help our clients attain pleasure and never to attain some unmeaningful goal such as $X$ number of orgasms per encounter.

As we mature more in our understanding of human sexuality, we realize that sex need not be an all-or-nothing event that, once begun, must lead to coitus. This point is especially important when counseling alcoholic clients and probably should be dealt with at length throughout treatment.

There are several reasons why the couple should be assisted in the discussion of their feelings and helped to broaden their views on sexual pleasure. First, insisting sexual contact must lead to coitus limits the opportunity for sexual pleasure and simple interaction. Although both sexes suffer pressure because of this faulty thinking, females seem to verbalize their concern more frequently. When a touch must lead to sexual intercourse, touching will become limited in its meaning and its use. The pleasure of a quick private caress, the understanding conveyed by the squeeze of a hand when others are present, the release of tension when the shoulders are rubbed are all lost because the intention may be misinterpreted. Even decidedly sexual touching need not lead to the next step. In our section on basic techniques, we will develop certain ways in which clients may learn to expand their opportunities for pleasure.

## THE COUNSELOR AS A RESOURCE

In sex counseling, the worker should function as a resource by (1) being familiar with the anatomy and physiology of males and females, (2) having a fund of counseling techniques to draw upon, and (3) being a model for teaching responsible and healthy attitudes about sexuality.

1. Familiarity with the anatomy and physiology pertaining to both sexes is the base upon which one develops sex counseling skills. With this solid information, the counselor must help the client dispel any mysteriousness surrounding sexual functioning before other treatment of specific sexual problems begins. Since many excellent books deal with sexual anatomy and physiology, we will not detail it here.

2. The counseling techniques must be simple to use, nonintrusive, and effective. Some basic techniques to modify sexual problem behavior are presented later in this chapter.

3. The counselor's role as model is very important to effective sex counseling. No technique is a substitute for the effect of the counselor's own open, responsible attitude toward sexuality. This attitude has a powerful impact on clients and should be considered part of the treatment.

Thinking, discussing, and clarifying her own feelings about sex is a necessary step for the counselor in preparing to help clients with their sexual problems. It is as necessary as the understanding of treatment technique.

Some counselors prefer private, informal discussions with one or two co-workers. Others find formal group discussions where opposing views are voiced beneficial in desensitizing themselves to the topic and in exposing them to views that may be alien to them. Most agree that reading manuals and literature on treatment technique also is important. The counselor might explore her feelings and attitudes about the topics in Table 12.

Sexual contact, despite all current attempts to distort it, is still best when based on love, caring, and efforts to share and understand. The goal of sex counseling is not to make a better machine but to give people the tools to love and care for one another. Just as we may hesitate to use slang so we may become uncomfortable in using terms of tenderness. We suggest that sexual pleasure is based on tenderness rather than exploitation, and the counselor, as the model, would be wise to use words with caring connotations.

We all have blind spots in our thinking for which all the logic we can muster will be insufficient to clear. In sex counseling, the use of an opposite sexed co-therapist will serve several purposes. First, each can be attuned to the other's blind spots and take over at that time; second, since ideally, couples will be seen, each may identify with the same sexed counselor and so lessen feelings of being victimized; third, each

| TABLE 12. | SEXUAL TOPICS FOR DISCUSSION BY COUNSELOR | |
|---|---|---|

1. prevailing moral attitude in the community
2. divorce
3. abortion
4. premarital sex and habitation
5. homosexuality, male and female
6. sex crimes, such as sexual assault, rape
7. extramarital sex
8. female sexuality
9. male sexuality
10. contraception
11. various positions in intercourse
12. use of various slang words
13. biracial couples
14. sexual expression in the older person
15. promiscuity
16. pornography
17. discussions of sexuality
18. women's rights movement
19. sharing of household duties

therapist may act as a model of how adults may relate to each other.

If the counselor can keep a sense of humor about this sometimes serious, sometimes laughable aspect of humanity, and if she can impart some of this humor to the clients, both counselor and client can benefit. Mistakes, misunderstandings, and negative feelings can be handled in a constructive manner.

## ASSESSMENT

### Areas To Investigate
The use of functional behavioral analysis will give the counselor information to determine the existence of sexual problems. During initial data gathering each area of the client's life is probed extensively enough to determine whether counseling is necessary. If a sexual problem is disclosed, more detailed information on this area is necessary. Below is a format (Table 13) adapted from several sources. This guide is useful in gathering information on the history of the sexual problem and the client's sexual experience. Having this information will be necessary in desensitizing the client to talk about sexuality and in beginning the teaching function that is a necessary part of sex counseling. The format follows a natural and relatively nonthreatening progression since it begins with early experiences.

*TABLE 13.*    *SEXUAL HISTORY*

Name:                          Address:

Date:                          Sex:

1. When and how did you first obtain knowledge about sex?
2. How did your parents handle questions and incidents concerning sex? What displays of affection did they make towards one another?
3. At what age were you first aware of sexual feelings?
4. At what age did you begin:
   a. menstruation
   b. breast enlargement
   c. development of pubic hairs
   d. voice change
   What were your feelings about these changes? Were there problems associated with them?
5. How did you feel about masturbation as a child? How often did you engage in this?
6. When did you start dating?
7. When did you have your first coital experience? Describe the situation.
8. Describe other relevant heterosexual and homosexual encounters.
9. Briefly describe your level of knowledge, attitudes, and morality concerning sex.
10. Describe your present partner(s) as to physical and emotional characteristics, type relationship you have, attitudes toward sex, etc.
11. What is the presenting problem?
12. What do you consider sexually arousing concerning:
    a. fantasies
    b. visual stimuli
    c. setting or environment
    d. attributes of partner
    e. technique and position
    f. dress
13. What form of contraception is used? Is it mutually satisfactory?
14. Please give any relevant information in the following areas:
    a. miscarriages or abortions
    b. sterilization performed

*Table 13, cont.*

    c. venereal disease
    d. sexual deviations
    e. experience with prostitutes
    f. extramarital experiences
15. What other information, that has not been covered, do you consider to be important?

---

### Asking Intimate Questions

In a recent National Institute on Alcohol Abuse and Alcoholism publication (NIAAA Information and Feature Services, 26 November, 1975),[3] a report on the workshop discussing how to deal with the client's sexual problems concludes by stating that such problems should be dealt with but that the *subject must be treated with great care to ward off offensiveness.*

When dealing in sensitive areas such as the sexual one, *how* questions are asked and comments are made becomes especially important. Clients are particularly sensitive to the hidden meaning that certain wordings may have. For example, "Did you ever masturbate?" certainly has a different meaning than does the question, "How old were you when you first masturbated?" Not only does the counselor get different information, but she also gives a different message to the client. We suggest there are several assumptions that the clients might make about each question. The former question may lead clients to assume that masturbation is unusual and that the counselor may have some negative feelings about it. Conversely, the latter question assumes that masturbation is a sexual experience that usually is engaged in by others and begins at an earlier age. With the aid of other questions worded in an accepting manner, the interview should develop into a free and open exchange on which counseling may be based.

Clients may obligingly offer the counselor the answer they think is wanted. There is less chance of this happening when the counselor refrains from offering alternative answers. For example, when the client did not answer the question "How often do you have intercourse?" the counselor suggested, "Once or twice a week?" The client quickly chose one of the limited alternatives. If the counselor feels she must prompt at all, she may get a more accurate response by giving a wider range of possible replies, "Once a month, once a day, once a year, once a week?"

Interviewers work with clients of various groups to which they may not belong, such as adolescents, retired people, and various ideological or religious groups. These clients may use idiosyncratic terms for body parts or sexual acts which are not a part of the counselor's vocabulary. Although the counselor should know or ask the client the meaning of these terms and be comfortable with the client's use of them, she need not incorporate them into her speech. We agree with Pomeroy[4] that to use the most technical language the clients know and are comfortable with for body parts and sexual acts helps establish a rapport based on mutual understanding and respect for each other. This calls for a sensitive testing on the part of the counselor who must base choice of words on an evaluation of the client's intelligence, socioeconomic level, and affiliation with a particular group. Using a technical term that is apt to be misunderstood by the clients is unwise. For example, "sexual intercourse" or simply "intercourse" is more readily understood by all groups than is "coitus."

Too, the counselor's use of words may indicate her attitude toward sex. Although there are advantages in using technical terms, sole reliance on them may be a way of distancing oneself from the development of a mature dialogue.

## BASIC TECHNIQUES

Basic techniques used in sex counsling are described in the following paragraphs. Some of these will be familiar, for they are used to remedy other problems.

### Sensate Focus

Many adults do not have available the ability to enjoy their partners in a physical but nonsexual manner. Perhaps some just have never learned; others have known but have lost it through neglect or discarded it because of punishment. The assumption that pleasurable touching must necessarily lead to intercourse is a societal distortion. The exercise of **sensate focus** allows the couple to give and get pleasure and explore each others' bodies in a purposefully nonsexual way. Social responsibility is removed, and the couple are specifically told to refrain from ejaculation and orgasm. Sensate focus is usually the first step in treatment. It is based on the following steps which are adapted from Masters and Johnson (1970).

1. One partner gives pleasure to the other by touching (other senses are involved peripherally at this point). However, the couple are told not to touch each other's genital area or the woman's breasts.

109

2. The partner who is receiving pleasure will stop the other from touching in a way that is uncomfortable or unpleasurable. This may be done verbally ("softer," "a bit harder") or nonverbally (moving the partner's hand).
3. The pleasuring partner has as his or her *second* goal the pleasuring of his/her partner. The *first* goal is to focus on his or her own pleasure at the discovery of the sensation of touching.
4. Finally, tasks are reversed.

The exercise is structured only as much as is needed by the individual couple. The counselor should instruct the couple to choose a time free from distractions and a private setting where they will be comfortable in undressing, for this task is best accomplished without the impediments of clothing. Some couples, however, may be so estranged that they will have to work up to this point. Some couples also may need for the counselor to designate length of time for the task. This can be done if it is clear that the couple need to begin at that point.

In using this exercise the counselor should be perceptive and fully discuss any fears or misgivings the couple may have. Generally the exercise is done at least three or four times before proceeding to the next phase. A counseling discussion centering on the couple's expectations and response should be held after the exercise. It will indicate if they are ready to proceed to the next phase of treatment.

### Sensate Focus B

The same steps are used, except in **Sensate Focus B** touching includes the genital areas and the woman's breasts. One goal of the exercise is to encourage the couple to view these areas as parts of the body, although sexual parts, rather than as entities that are somewhat removed and having special meaning. The other goals in this exercise include: lifting responsibility for sexual performance, giving and receiving pleasure in a relaxed, exploring manner, and letting each partner teach the other not only what is pleasurable but also *what* is being pleasured. The authors have had success in using this exercise in an educational and responsibility-free manner by suggesting that each partner when acting as the pleasure-giver assume he or she knows nothing of the other's anatomy while the other names the part being touched ("My penis feels warm when you rub it." "I am aware of your stroking my clitoris.")

### Self-Stimulation

Self-stimulation (Annon[5] prefers to use the term "self-exploration" with clients) is the self-directed use of masturbation to teach oneself what is pleasurable and arousing and how to experience orgasm. Approximation procedures are an important aspect of self-stimulation. Stepwise, at a pace comfortable to the client, new sexual behaviors, including orgasm with a partner, are learned. Negative attitudes towards one's body are changed as the client learns the ability to pleasure oneself. Eventually, the client will be able to teach his partner what is pleasing. Steps for teaching self-stimulation follow: (1) A full explanation and discussion with appropriate literature is the first step. (2) The client is requested to refrain from sexual intercourse temporarily so that he is not under pressure to perform. (3) The client is instructed to choose a private place and time and to view his body in a mirror, concentrating on aspects which are pleasing. A hand mirror should be used to explore the genital area. Familiarization is important and should be done thoroughly. (4) Next, as in sensate focus, the client touches, rubs, caresses his body, concentrating on the feeling as he lightly, then more deliberately touches each part. (5) The client is taught through explanations during counseling sessions and literature how to stimulate the genitals to excitement. Pictures are useful as the counselor describes the quick pumping action of the penis, clitoris, and vagina. Vibrators may be recommended, especially for female clients.

Often clients stop just short of orgasm for fear of losing control or exploding. They should be encouraged to move at their own pace, explaining the naturalness of these feelings and what can be expected. Any attempts at self-stimulation are rewarded by interest and pleasure. It is expected that as the client experiences the pleasant bodily sensations he will want more pleasure and find it easier to attempt.

Once orgasm can be attained through self-stimulation, the client will teach the partner. At first, manual stimulation is used. When both are ready, coitus may then be learned in the same fashion.

As mentioned earlier, it is preferable to use a term other than masturbation since objectionable meanings are associated with it. Usually, however, if the technique is prescribed matter-of-factly, the client raises no objections.

## Fantasy

Most people seem to think that the use of fantasy during coitus is wrong, somehow disloyal to one's partner. There is less difficulty in requesting a client to use fantasy during self-stimulation. Most writers think that fantasy has a legitimate place in both self-stimulation and in coitus. There seems to be a large segment of sexually adequate people who do fantasize. Often, when one partner is aroused, the other might use fantasy to achieve arousal so that she may become actively involved in the giving and getting of sexual pleasure.

Clients who have difficulty fantasizing may be trained in the counseling sessions. The easiest method is to use appropriate pictures, having the client alternate between viewing the picture and closing her eyes briefly, attempting to hold the image. Clients will find they can hold the image for greater lengths of time until they are able to evoke the image without benefit of the picture. Fantasy may be used in several ways. There are reports of successful treatment of various sexual problems through the use of masturbatory fantasy. If clients have difficulty with this, discussion and practice are usually adequate to prepare them to use this aid to sexual engagement.

## Attitude Change

Very often the client has negative attitudes and feelings toward sex based on misinformation, previous negative experiences, lack of knowledge, and/or dislike or anger toward the sexual partner. In most instances, it is necessary to change such attitudes prior to active treatment to obtain the client's full cooperation. An example of aversion based on previous negative experience is that of a young woman who would not become involved with men for fear they would become sexually aggressive and disregard her wishes. She had been molested as a young adolescent and had not had opportunity to resolve her feelings about the incident. She had developed a fear of arousal that caused her to avoid potentially sexual encounters. Attitude change became one part of her treatment.

## Desensitization

**Desensitization** is the gradual lessening of anxiety associated with a thought or act. Desensitization may be accomplished through familiarization (either in real life or fantasy) or slow approximation to the goal. Sensate focus (already discussed) is a basic technique used to desensitize clients to their bodies and sexuality. Other ways of sexually desensitizing a client is through discussion of sexuality, reading of certain literature, and assignment of simple nonthreatening tasks.

## Social-Skills Training

Sexual skills must overlie basic social skills for obvious reasons. Especially with the alcoholic clients who may have neglected social skills, the counselor should make a thorough check during the assessment procedure. The need for social skills is evident in the couple who may come together in coitus for quick sexual release but who have not had a pleasant conversation in years. See Chapter 6.

112

## Assertion Training

Although a part of social skills, assertiveness is given special note here because many clients with sexual problems need assertion training. Men and women who find it difficult to request certain kinds of sexual contact with their partners are prime targets for assertion training. See Chapter 5.

## Home Tasks

A major part of sex counseling is the assignment of home tasks. Counseling sessions are used to discuss feelings, explain tasks, and obtain feedback. Because the tasks are carried out at home, it is extremely important that the counselor fully explain the procedure and rationale of the task. It is best to write out steps to accomplish the task so that clients may refer to them for clarification. Also, it should be expected that clients will keep a written record of their assignments. Form 4 is a sample form which may be given to the clients.

## SEXUAL PROBLEMS IN THE FEMALE

Just as the male has been burdened with the responsibility for action in sexual matters so the female has had the responsibility for restraining possible action. As a girl reaches sexual maturity, she is told that *she* must "set the limits" sexually and should realize that boys "cannot control themselves." These warnings, given throughout adolescence, contribute to many a female's inability to enjoy sexual relationships and the development of a fear of, or dislike for, males. Ironically, these women are expected to perform adequately and enjoy sexual contact under certain restricted conditions, for example, after marriage.

The basis for treatment of female sexual dysfunction is a re-education of the woman and her partner. The misconceptions concerning female sexuality must be uncovered and corrected. A list of the most prevalent misconceptions (Table 14) is offered so that the counselor may become alert to them.

Feelings of sexuality are based on a person's self-concept. If the self-concept is poor, attempts to make one feel good about the sexual self is futile. Feminists have begun to question mental health workers about their attitudes toward women and the kind of expectations they convey to their female clients. This same atmosphere of re-evaluation has begun in the treatment of female alcoholics. Previously, an alcoholic woman was assumed to have negative feelings about her sex and sexuality. Counselors now evaluate the individual to determine the problem areas specific to her, rather than make general statements about her problems. The counselor will attempt a determination based

FORM 4.  HOME TASK INFORMATION

Client's Name:

| Date | Time | | Place | Task | Outcome |
|------|------|------|-------|------|---------|
|      | To   | From |       |      |         |
|      |      |      |       |      |         |
|      |      |      |       |      |         |
|      |      |      |       |      |         |
|      |      |      |       |      |         |

on the client's personal data. Direct sexual training alone is insufficient. It must be augmented by treatment of such issues as religious difficulties, passivity, poor skills, inhibition in expression of feelings, discomfort with one's own body, anger toward men, and fear of men, sex, and insertion of the penis.

Some criticism must be made of the great amount of literature concerning *sex role conflicts in alcoholic females.* Perhaps always a less-than-valid concept, it is especially so in the present time when women are exploring their roles and developing ones which are more acceptable to them. Again, a warning might be given to the counselor lest he interpret sexual problems as a rejection of the woman's femaleness.

The following is a discussion of treatment of the major sexual problems of the female.

## Orgasmic Dysfunction

Orgasmic dysfunction may be primary or secondary in nature. A woman is said to have **primary orgasmic dysfunction** if she has never

TABLE 14.    SOME COMMON MISCONCEPTIONS
                     CONCERNING SEXUALITY

*Concerning Males*

1. They can perform no matter who the partner is or what the setting is.

2. Their sex drive is so high they cannot control themselves once aroused.

3. They cannot be tender and gentle unless there is a problem with masculinity.

4. They instinctively know how to please a woman.

5. Their ego will be hurt if a woman becomes assertive sexually.

*Concerning Females*

1. They don't enjoy sex and weren't intended to.

2. They have a low sex drive.

3. They are innately passive unless they have difficulty with their role as women.

4. True women have vaginal rather than clitoral orgasms.

5. They want to be sexually dominated.

---

achieved orgasm under any circumstances. **Secondary orgasmic dysfunction** indicates the client has experienced orgasm either through vaginal or rectal intercourse, oral-genital stimulation, self-stimulation, or partner manipulations. The following treatment has been most successful.

1. The client and her partner are reassured that the problem can be corrected. The initial sessions are used to educate the couple on physiological and psychological aspects of sexuality, develop open communication, and reverse any misconceptions about sexuality.

2. The client is requested to refrain from coitus temporarily.

3. She is taught how to bring herself to orgasm through self-stimulation. This process is described in an earlier section.

4. Probably concurrently with Step 3, assertiveness is developed in the client so that she will request from the partner what will give

115

her pleasure. There are women who feel it is not their place to make requests of their partners. A discussion of such attitudes and training in how to request would be necessary.

5. Sensate Focus A and B are used in a transitional step from self-stimulation to partner-stimulation.
6. The partners position themselves for intercourse. The woman places the penis against her genitals and when ready, near her vagina. At all times she is in control of the procedure, moving only as quickly as she wishes.
7. Continuing Step 6, she takes the penis into the vaginal opening. The male is instructed not to thrust but to allow his partner to move as she wills. Gradually, more of the penis is taken in.
8. She is instructed to experience the sensations of having the penis in her vagina and to determine what position is most pleasurable to her.
9. She is to instruct her partner about the pleasurable sensations she experiences and what she would like him to do so that she may have an orgasm.

The partner must fully understand the program and be willing to forego pleasure temporarily. If he cannot control ejaculation, he probably should be prepared to remove the penis. Many women take this as a lack of interest in their problem so that discussion is necessary before beginning the program.

In some parts of the country, women who are nonorgasmic are treated in groups with good results. The steps are essentially the same as those just given, with the additional value of sharing experiences with others having the same difficulty.

## Vaginismus

Vaginismus is a psychophysiological difficulty which prevents the woman from completing intercourse. There is a spastic contraction of the muscles of the perineum and outer third of the vagina. It is an involuntary reflex initiated by imagined, anticipated, or actual attempts at vaginal entry. Assessment includes history and pelvic examination.

Masters and Johnson (1970) have obtained excellent results over a period of time using the following treatment.

1. Sensitive discussion of the disorder helps both partners understand that the contractions are involuntary.
2. Desensitization of the vaginal opening is accomplished by the insertion of dilators of graduated size. The woman may insert the dilator with the assistance of her partner and gradually allow the partner more control while she verbally directs the insertion.

3. Upon mutual consent, the couple attempt gradual insertion of the penis. This may or may not require gradual steps as with the dilators.

## Female Dyspareunia

Female dyspareunia denotes pain either during or subsequent to intercourse. Cause may be physiological (infection, endometreosis, cysts, poor lubrication) psychological, or a combination of the two. Cause is often difficult to ascertain, and physical causes may be ruled out arbitrarily. A complete history and pelvic and rectal examination by competent personnel are necessary. Even then, misdiagnosis is possible. The following is a description of treatment for the most common causes of dyspareunia.

*Infection* may be caused by fungus such as Monilia. Sometimes infection occurs from rectal intercourse or contact with clothing or other foreign bodies. Treatment with antibiotics and education to avoid future infection are necessary.

*Sensitivity reactions* to such agents as contraceptive foams, pills, condoms, diaphragms, douches, or bath preparations can cause an itching or burning sensation that may lead to chronic dyspareunia. Detection of cause and discontinuation of the chemical are often all that is necessary.

*Inadequate vaginal lubrication* may be due to lack of interest at that time or with that particular partner; fear of coitus, pregnancy, or something else causing the woman to remain uninvolved; or postmenopausal atrophy. The last, *post-menopausal atrophy*, is best treated by sex-steroid-replacement therapy.

When there is lack of interest, the condition may be transitory, as in instances when the woman is preoccupied or finds her partner unappealing for some reason. Inadequate vaginal lubrication at such times may be likened to the male's inability to achieve erection for similar reasons.

*Fear* sometimes stems from a traumatic incident, such as rape or sexual molestation. Chronic insufficiency of lubrication caused by such fear can be treated in the following way.

1. The fear should be discussed by counselor and client.
2. Desensitization can be accomplished through counseling and sensate focus exercises with the desired partner.
3. The woman should learn how to develop arousal; the partner also should learn what can be done to arouse the woman. Setting and timing as well as touching, kissing, and all other aspects of foreplay allow for arousal to develop. Too little foreplay is the com-

117

plaint most often raised by women.

4. The use of fantasy to arouse oneself is also taught as in the previous section.

*Lack of interest* is a particularly serious problem of the alcoholic couple. Sexual abuse and rape of the woman by the alcoholic partner is a problem which should be given special attention. The woman who finds herself in such a situation is a likely candidate for sexual problems. The situation may be beyond repair, and the only practical solution may be separation or divorce. However, if the couple wishes counseling or if the situation is not as deteriorated, treatment based on the various problem areas is recommended. Until a degree of mutual respect and understanding can be developed through counseling, the couple should be advised to refrain from sexual contact.

Once communication lines are established, basic problems are reconciled, and the alcoholism is under control, counseling may include sexual dysfunction, if these problems have not reconciled themselves. Sex counseling, then, would start with sensate focus as a kind of getting-reacquainted period. Treatment would continue as with other insufficient lubrication causes if this is still a problem.

## General Lack Of Sexual Interest

General lack of sexual interest usually exists in the presence of other more specific sexual dysfunction. It is said to exist when either or both partners describe a discrepancy between actual as opposed to desired sexual encounter. Traditionally, it has been assumed that women simply had a weaker sex drive than did men. We now know that lack of sexual interest is due to other reasons which include fear or dislike of sex based on bad experience, misinformation, marital or other personal problems, depression, physiological difficulty, and lack of knowledge about her own sexuality and about how to obtain pleasure. In general, however, lack of sexual interest may be said to be caused by a low return as compared to high investment of energy, time, and emotionality. When these circumstances are present, the woman will avoid sexual encounters. Accurate assessment of causes for disinterest is essential. Goal of treatment will be to balance more equitably the cost-return of sexual encounters.

The case of June B. illustrates the complexity which this problem may encompass. June is 32 years old, married, mother of two children, and working as office manager for a mental health program. Having a high school diploma and one semester in college, she has risen to her present position in the 10 months she has been with the program. This is her first job in five years. She receives much attention and many compliments on her work. Her self-confidence, always poor, is beginning to increase.

June's husband, Arthur, also bright, has not been able to succeed so well in his work because of his alcohol problem. When he is home, he is the center of the family, and he meets his need for success by an authoritarian stand. When June began work, this changed. She shared work incidents with the family, thus taking some attention away from her husband. She spent less time on household chores and requested assistance from Arthur and the children and, even then, appeared tired at times. Worst of all in Arthur's eyes, June began talking about obtaining a college education. Arthur became frightened and, as is likely to happen at such times, did all the wrong things. He complained, tried to restrict June, and insisted she quit work. Through all this, the couple were able to maintain their sexual relationship.

June finally quit her job. She became despondent, and she neglected herself and her family. When her husband complained, she became hostile. Unable to cope, he began to drink heavily. They avoided each other whenever possible, including sexually. When they finally sought assistance, the counselor discovered a relationship that had been outgrown, a fearful husband who refused to consider change, a wife who felt stifled and thereby threatened her husband, and a sexual relationship showing the effects of their other problems. Until the couple can get to a point where they are willing to work on their problems and compromise with one another, the sexual relationship will be strained. However, once they begin to work together, sexual involvement most likely will help them become close again.

As with other aspects of counseling, timing is important. A client must be ready to consider a problem and changes. To begin in areas which are least threatening seems the best strategy.

## SEXUAL PROBLEMS IN THE MALE

Our society places great responsibilities on the male. Even with changing attitudes, the male is still seen as necessarily the initiator of sexual encounters and what is worse, the partner who makes the sexual relationship good or bad. An important part of sexual counseling with the alcoholic male and his partner is the development of an understanding that no person should or could take this much responsibility. Mutuality of responsibility is a key to a good sexual relationship. As the counselor and client progress with the interview, the client's views and beliefs will emerge. It is necessary that the counselor gently question beliefs that seem erroneous and a possible source of conflict. In this section we will discuss the most prevalent sexual dysfunctions of the alcoholic male.

## Impotency Of The Male

Male impotency is the inability to attain or sustain an erection to the completion of coitus or to the satisfaction of both the man and his partner. **Impotence** may be either **primary** (the male has never been able to attain or sustain an erection sufficient to accomplish coitus) or **secondary** (at least one instance of successful entry). Most men experience occasional erection failure, especially when fatigued or distracted. Masters and Johnson (1970) do not diagnose impotency unless the male's failure rate is about 25 percent of his attempts. Causes include aging, systemic disorders, sociological and psychological difficulties, interpersonal problems associated with his partner, female sexual dysfunction, alcohol, and other drugs (prescribed or nonprescribed).

Alcohol may act temporarily as a sexual stimulant. However, its chronic overuse can destroy the male's sexual ability. Although a gradual return may be expected after several months' abstinence, there is evidence that in some instances the dysfunction is irreversible. Certain drugs (for example, Librium) also may have such an effect on sexual ability, though reversible. Lay people are usually unaware of these effects. Part of the treatment package, then, is to educate clients to such matters.

Masters and Johnson state the three primary goals in the treatment of male impotence as:

1. Removal of the male's fears of sexual performance.
2. Reorientation of behavioral patterns so that he becomes an active participant rather than remains in his usual role of spectator.
3. Relief of the partner's fears about the male's sexual performance.

The expectation that males can perform whenever and where desired is erroneous. At one time or another, this expectation is a source of difficulty for most males. In removing these expectations and responsibilities and in focusing, rather, on the male's giving pleasure to his partner, the impotency is treated by a kind of nontreatment. Any planning for erection is placing on the client the expectation that an erection will occur. Any male knows that the mere willing is not enough.

The philosophy of sexual contact with a loved one is important. The losing of oneself in the pleasure of the other allows attention to be removed from oneself. Using many ways to give pleasure lessens the importance of the penis so that pressure of performance is removed. Sessions in which the couple learn of the many aspects of sexual pleasure apart from intercourse form a basis for treatment.

Dr. Arnold Lazarus uses assertion training of the client to help the male become an active participant.[6] Dr. Lazarus views sexual inability as part of a pattern of nonassertive behavior and feelings of threat when expected to assume a sexually assertive demeanor. By specific training, the individual may give overt expression to sexual feelings that have been inhibited in the past.

Dr. Lazarus spends some time discussing the unattractiveness of such passive behavior and its various negative repercussions, including sexual and other problems. Next, the client is taught how to be assertive in various situations (See Chapter 5, Assertion Training). The client keeps a detailed record of all sexual attempts and outcomes. It is necessary that the client knows failure is expected but more success will come with time and training. At each session, the feelings and responses associated with the last week's attempts are discussed.

A modification of Lazarus' technique is the use of assertion training in conjunction with sensate focus and mutual stimulation exercises. Treatment may be slower since the clients are to refrain from coitus, but the sense of failure is lessened.

## Premature Ejaculation

*Definition and causes.* There are several definitions of premature ejaculation based on duration. These seem inadequate when taking into account the interpersonal aspects of coitus. As with other pleasures, criterion is an individual matter. For our purposes, a definition of premature ejaculation must take into account the requirements of the man and his partner. Therefore, the following definition will be used: A client suffers from the syndrome of premature ejaculation if he cannot control the ejaculating process for sufficient duration after intravaginal containment to satisfy his partner in at least half of their coital unions (Masters and Johnson, 1970). The figure is necessarily arbitrary and will change according to the partner's expectations. If the partner is non-orgasmic for reasons other than rapid ejaculation of the male, the assessment of premature ejaculation is inappropriate.

The complaintant usually is the female who feels the frustration of sexual tension that is not released. The sexual double standard is glaringly evident here. Cultural misconceptions about human sexuality have led to relationships in which the male may not even realize the woman's needs and in which the woman, frustrated though she may be, is afraid to state her needs for fear of being labeled "unwomanly" and "castrating."

Some sociocultural causes for premature ejaculation are guilt feelings associated with sexual activity, leading the client to try to achieve orgasm quickly; and the use of withdrawal as a contraceptive measure that relies on peak excitement, a few rapid intravaginal thrusts, and quick withdrawal. This results in ejaculation and release for the male but frustration for the female since few couples attempt sexual tension release for her by such techniques as manual stimulation.

*Treatment.* If sexual interaction is to be a pleasurable experience rather than a tolerated one and be considered another aspect of a good interpersonal relationship, the needs of the female partner also must be met. Education must focus on the mutuality of the sex act and needs and responsibilities of both partners. *Assertion training* for the female may teach her to ask for various pleasures and to show the partner how to please her. *Information* on sexuality will teach both partners the needs of the woman and the controls available to the man.

Some traditional ways males have attempted to delay ejaculation include distracting attention from the act to thoughts and images that are nonerotic, concentrating on pain such as biting one's lips, using depressants such as alcohol or barbiturates, and using anesthetic ointments or several condoms in an attempt to reduce tactile stimulation. All these have met with questionable success.

Success rate for reversibility of this syndrome is quite high, given proper treatment. The most widely accepted is the **squeeze technique** developed by James Semans.[7] It is based on the fact that when sufficient pressure is applied to the penis, the male will lose his urge to ejaculate. The procedure adapted from Masters and Johnson (1970) is outlined below:

1. A description of the two stages of the male orgasmic response (Stage 1: ejaculatory inevitability; Stage 2: involuntary expulsion of seminal fluid content) is given the couple. Thorough descriptions may be found in sex manuals.
2. During the sensate-focus exercises at home, the partner is encouraged to touch, stroke, and fondle the penis and other genitals and the entire pelvic area of the male. Done over a series of sessions, the result should be a desensitization to this kind of touching and a readiness for the next phase of treatment.
3. The couple should position themselves in such a way so that the partner will have full access to the male's genital organs. It is suggested that he lie with his legs apart and the partner sit between his legs.
4. In this position, the partner caresses the male's penis to cause erection.
5. Upon full erection, the partner begins the squeeze technique. Correct position of fingers and strong pressure are necessary. The partner's thumb is placed on the frenulum (located on the lower

surface of the penis on the coronal ridge), and the *first* and *second* fingers are placed on the upper surface of the penis immediately above and below the coronal ridge. The partner squeezes the thumb and both fingers together for only 3 to 4 seconds. With sufficient pressure approximately 25 percent of the erection will be lost.

6. After approximately half a minute of release, the partner resumes penile caressing until full erection is achieved at which time the squeeze technique is again used.

7. Alternately, the penis is allowed to reach full erection and then is squeezed to impede ejaculation. This is repeated four or five times during the initial session.

Goals for this phase are the development of communication, development of ejaculation control under conditions of sexual excitement, and encouragement of the man and his partner to develop positive expectations for treatment.

In the next phase vaginal containment is employed in a non-demanding manner.

8. The previous steps are done several times as practice.

9. The female then mounts her partner, positioning herself so that she can insert the penis and move back on it.

10. The penis is contained in a motionless manner so that the male may desensitize himself and remain in control of the erection. Aware that his partner will not begin pelvic thrusting, he may relax and experience the sensation of containment.

11. If the male feels he will lose his control, he communicates this to his partner who quickly moves forward off the penis and uses the squeeze technique for 3-4 seconds.

12. Insertion is again accomplished and Steps 10 and 11 are alternated as necessary.

The next phase, entered when the man is ready, successively approximates the full aspect of sexual intercourse, including pelvic thrusting.

13. The previous steps are completed. The female remains motionless, allowing the male at his own pace to make tentative easy thrusts and moves.

14. When he communicates impending loss of control, his partner quickly uses the squeeze technique then reinserts the penis.

15. Slowly, as the couple gain more confidence, freer motion will occur.

The couple should realize that occasional failure simply means temporarily reverting back to the squeeze technique.

## Lack Of Sexual Interest Of Male

Lack of sexual interest of the male has the same etiology as lack of interest of the female. Fear of failure, poor interpersonal relationship with his partner, and sexual dysfunction can be involved. And as with the female, the generalized reason for lack of interest is poor payoff compared to cost. Full assessment of cause is necessary. The client should be released from demand pressures by a statement that sexual intercourse cease temporarily.

The alcoholic male is especially prone to sexual dysfunction because of long-term alcohol use and interpersonal problems. The incidence of impotence while drinking is high. When this happens, the client may avoid all sexual encounters. Usually the alcoholic, male or female, must re-learn how to communicate, relate, and develop an intimate relationship as well as remedy sexual problems.

## Footnotes

1. R. Cantanzaro, ed., *Alcoholism: The total treatment approach.* Springfield, IL: Charles C. Thomas, Publisher, 1974.

2. W. H. Masters and V. E. Johnson. *Human sexual inadequacy.* Boston: Little, Brown, 1970.

3. NIAAA information and feature service. Workshop series deals with client sex problems, November 26, 1975.

4. W. B. Pomeroy. The sex interview in counseling. In Mary S. Calderone, ed., *Sexuality and human values.* New York: Association Press, 1974.

5. J. Annon. The extension of learning principles to the analysis of treatment of sexual problems. *Dissertation Abstracts International,* 1971, *32,* 362.

6. A. N. Lazarus. Modes of treatment for sexual inadequacies. *Medical Aspects of Human Sexuality,* 1969, *3,* 53-58.

7. J. H. Semans. Premature ejaculation: A new approach. *Southern Medical Journal,* 1956, *49,* 353-357.

---

Permission for the material in this chapter concerning treatment of sexual inadequacies in males (impotency, premature ejaculation) and females (nonorgasmic dysfunction, dysmenorrhea, vaginismus) was cordially granted by Dr. William H. Masters and Virginia E. Johnson, from *Human Sexual Inadequacy,* Boston: Little, Brown, 1970.

# 8 Self-Control Training

*DEFINING SELF-CONTROL AND SELF-MANAGEMENT*

Although the term self-control has various meanings in our society, it is usually associated with an individual's will power. For example, laymen and even professionals often describe the alcoholic's succumbing to temptation after a period of abstinence as being a lack of will power. Actually this term is very vague. To be more precise, we will use the phrase **self-control** to denote activity (either behavioral or cognitive) of an individual which leads to improvement in the behavior of that same person. Defined in this way, self-control is perceived as a skill that can be developed through practice.

Self-control, then, takes on a very special meaning. The term **self-management** which is often used interchangeably with self-control probably represents a more accurate description of what is involved. The client is essentially managing his own behavior. For example, let's suppose that Fred R., a heavy drinker, has not had a drink in two weeks. He is trying very hard not to be tempted to drink. Actually what we mean by being tempted is being exposed to those cues in the environment that have precipitated heavy drinking in the past. Fred has been very likely to drink in the time interval after work and before he gets home. Usually the friends that Fred rides home with will stop for "a drink or two" and discuss the day's work. To gain self-control over this temptation, Fred arranges to (1) leave all of his money (except an amount needed for lunch) and credit cards at home, (2) ride home with a friend who does not drink, and (3) take his son fishing immediately after work. This may seem like self-control overkill, but Fred has made certain that the likelihood of his drinking is decreased. He has successfully removed the cues that serve as temptation: social pressure from friends, ready access to money, and no scheduled activity for the time immediately after work. In essence, one aspect of self-management consists of prearranging conditions that have been associated with drinking.

125

Another obvious way in which alcoholics practice self-control is through the use of Antabuse, a medication that is ingested once a day. Drinking after ingesting Antabuse results in nausea, vomiting, heart palpitations, and generally a very unpleasant experience. By taking Antabuse each morning the alcoholic is controlling temptation for the rest of the day.

Many clients inherently feel positive about self-management training since the control of their behavior is being placed in their own hands. Therefore, the counselor can simply explain the rationale for these procedures to the client without resorting to special techniques to sell the client on them. Prior to training, the client must be taught to functionally analyze her own behavior as we discussed in Chapter 2. The client must become more aware of the relationship between her drinking and specific cues around her. One method that appears to facilitate this awareness is discussing these relationships in a group therapy setting. Each member of the group can begin to associate specific behaviors with specific social-environmental events and to learn from feedback and suggestions provided by others.

## COMPONENTS OF SELF-MANAGEMENT TRAINING

Basically, self-management training consists of teaching four skills:

1. self-monitoring
2. rearranging environmental *cues*
3. rearranging environmental *consequences*
4. rearranging cues and consequences through cognitive events

### Self-Monitoring

Probably the most basic method of gaining control of behavior is through self-monitoring. This procedure requires the individual to record either the frequency or duration of his behavior. In Chapter 2 we discussed the use of self-monitoring as an assessment procedure. Self-monitoring can provide useful information on the functional relationships associated with drinking. We also know, from studies of substance abuse, that keeping track of one's own behavior serves to change that behavior. One way for the counselor to observe this phenomenon is to choose a behavior he himself wants to change. For example, he might want to decrease his smoking or eating behavior or increase his attention to unpleasant paper work on the job. Once he has chosen the behavior, he would define it behaviorally in terms of frequency, amount, or duration. If he chooses eating, he might decide to monitor the amount he eats at each meal or per day. Or, he would count calories. With cigarettes he would count the number smoked daily.

Now, for one week, he should keep an index card with him and begin to keep track of the behavior. He would keep a graph of his progress, probably noting as the week goes on, that the behavior is changing as a function of the self-monitoring. He also will notice that he is becoming more aware of the circumstances in which he is most likely to engage in that behavior. Thus, he is gaining increased control over his behavior through additional information and continual feedback to himself.

Now, how does a counselor specifically apply this technique to an alcoholic's problems? Essentially, this procedure can be applied to any behavior the client is trying to either increase or decrease. Drinking is an obvious one to be decreased. If the client is completely abstinent, however, there is no behavior for him to monitor at that particular time. In this case the counselor would have him monitor other behaviors related to drinking. For example, the number of urges to drink, the number of times he interacts with heavy drinking friends, or the number of self-derogatory thoughts ("What's the use, I might as well get drunk and forget about these problems" or "What's the use, things are just as bad whether I'm drunk or sober"). The client can also monitor positive behaviors that serve as alternatives to alcohol abuse. These might include the number of times that he effectively copes with a difficult interpersonal encounter or the number of times he engages in social interaction.

Self-monitoring as a feedback procedure to the client can be enhanced through graphing. Data can be graphically represented and discussed at therapy sessions. Frequently, clients are requested to display the graph in a conspicuous place at home. This public display serves as a motivating factor in behavior change since others become more aware of changes in behavior and, hence, are better able to recognize the client's efforts. Graphs also allow the client to observe slight positive changes in his behavior that may not be apparent from a more global view. In addition, graphs help to pinpoint the specific times and circumstances during which behavior improves or becomes disrupted. This allows both client and counselor to examine these circumstances and to use this information in formulating further therapeutic plans.

## Rearranging Environmental Cues

A variety of circumstances occur *prior to* a drinking episode. After the client has monitored her behavior and has functionally analyzed her past heavy drinking bouts, both she and the counselor should be better able to delineate specific cues which precipitate drinking. As we mentioned earlier, these cues include cognitive, social, emotional, situational, and physiological events. One major aim of treatment is to break up the relationship between these events and drinking behavior. There are two ways to accomplish this: (1) to teach the client more effective methods of dealing with these events (i.e., via more adaptive coping skills) or (2) to teach the client methods of modifying or rearranging these events. The first goal involves training that we have previously discussed (e.g., assertion training, social-skills training). The present chapter focuses on the latter skill, namely, self-management.

The counselor must be careful in helping the client decide which cues will be rearranged. Global issues, such as the effects that this rearrangement would have on the client's life, must be considered. One method of rearranging cues, and perhaps the simplest way, is to avoid them, as Fred did in the first example of this chapter. Following are three other example cases of cue avoidance, each one illustrating different degrees of possible negative side effects.

*Case No. 1.* John B. is a 45-year-old factory worker who has a 10-year history of excessive drinking. His typical drinking pattern in the past has been to stop off after work at one of the numerous bars along his route home. He usually would come home to his family two or three hours late in a very intoxicated state. Along with other therapeutic procedures, John might develop a self-management plan with his counselor in which he would avoid certain routes home from work that are heavily arrayed with taverns he has frequented in the past. We are making the assumption that the sight of these bars, because of past associations, will set off a chain of events which may lead to a drinking episode. Thus, alternative routes would be planned to allow John to avoid these cues. Now, the negative side effects of such a plan would be minimal. John may have to take a longer route home and may arrive 10 minutes later, but the major benefits would outweigh these minor inconveniences.

*Case No. 2.* Sarah G. is a 39-year-old widow with no children. She has been drinking heavily for five years. Her husband was wealthy and she is well off financially. Sarah does not work and spends a great deal of time by herself. Her only interaction with others comes from two or three alcoholic friends who frequently visit her for a drink. They usually end up going out for the evening together and drinking very heavily. One possible cue rearrangement for Sarah is to avoid all interactions with her alcoholic friends. This would certainly reduce a major precipitant of her drinking. However, the counselor must examine what else this might do to Sarah. First, it would essentially remove all of her sources of interpersonal satisfactions. Second, and related to the first, it probably would increase boredom and loneliness, which might not only precipitate drinking but also lead to severe depression. This is not to say, however, that the planned self-management strategy was poor and should not be undertaken. The counselor must also consider the timing of such intervention. That is, before removing these individuals as social cues, more appropriate social interactions, i.e., with nonalcoholic friends, must be initiated and developed (Participating in AA might be a good interim measure). In the meantime, Sarah can be taught ways of dealing with her alcoholic friends when they pressure her to drink (see Chapter 5). Then, she can sever her relationships with these friends if they continue to be a source of temptation to her. Rearranging cues must be timed properly and might not be advisable until alternative life styles are developed.

*Case No. 3.* Paul B. is a 35-year-old businessman who has periodic drinking binges, which are becoming more and more frequent. His drinking bouts are usually precipitated by conflicts with other people. Paul is a very nice person who has difficulty in saying no to people. For example, John S., one of Paul's acquaintances, is constantly asking Paul for money and not paying him back. In addition, John is a rather obnoxious character who seems to enjoy belittling Paul (through sarcastic remarks) when they are in a group. John's behavior toward Paul has frequently precipitated Paul's drinking binges. As a self-management procedure, should the counselor plan with Paul ways in which he could avoid John and thus rearrange a cue to his drinking? This may, of course, lessen the likelihood of Paul's becoming angry and hurt by John's actions. But, this would not be a very good therapeutic procedure for two reasons: (1) it is very unlikely that Paul will be able to avoid all interactions with John and (2) in addition to teaching Paul self-management skills through this procedure, this would also teach him to avoid solving problems in a direct, adaptive manner. This would not be therapeutic for Paul and may actually encourage his assertiveness deficits. In this situation Paul would be taught more appropriate ways to confront John through social-skills or assertion training (see Chapter 5). Rearranging cues through avoidance would *not* be indicated.

Situational cues that can be modified most readily include those related to time, place, person, and situation. After a functional analysis of drinking, certain dangerous time periods usually stand out. These are times when drinking is much more likely. This interval might be from 5 to 7 p.m. and from 10 a.m. to 12 noon. A housewife might be most likely to drink in mid-afternoon when she is alone. With respect to these intervals, clients can be taught to schedule other activities that are incompatible with excessive drinking. Thus, the client, with the aid of the counselor, writes out a specific schedule of possible activities. It is helpful to request the client to initially write down all of the potential activities that would make drinking unlikely or impossible.

The manner in which this is accomplished is illustrated in the case of Bob W. Bob is a 42-year-old married businessman with two children. The most likely times for him to drink excessively are immediately after work from 5:30 to 7:30 p.m. and in the evening before bedtime. Bob's counselor has requested him to jot down a list of activities that would make it difficult for him to drink during these times. Bob's list is divided into the two problem intervals of time he has identified. His list includes the following:

1. Eat supper immediately upon arrival home ("I never want a drink after eating").
2. Take my wife and children or wife alone out to supper, movie, or shopping.
3. Visit my sister and brother-in-law or friends (Bill and Marge), none of whom drink alcohol.
4. Work with my sons on restoring an "antique" car that I bought for them.
5. Read alcoholism literature.

*11 to 12:30 p.m. (Before bedtime)*

1. Arrange to have special intimate talks with my wife during this time.
2. Schedule nightly jogging from 11 to 11:30 p.m. ("I seldom feel like a drink after exercise").
3. Practice relaxation taught to me by the counselor to help me relax and sleep well.

Bob's list is fairly good, and the counselor praises his efforts at completing the assignment. The next step is to schedule specific activities that Bob will plan to engage in at these times during the next week. A number of alternatives should be available at any one time. To plan this schedule for himself, Bob must discuss it with his family and enlist their cooperation. For example, he might ask his wife to arrange to have the family supper early some nights, i.e., as soon as he arrives home from work. This might involve some rearranging or even compromise, such as his fixing the supper on one or two nights. In fact, Bob's preparing and serving supper one evening might fill in a considerable gap of time, providing an excellent incompatible activity.

Another cue is the situation or circumstance of drinking. In the case mentioned above, for example, Bob may have difficulty with temptations to drink at lunch time. As a businessman going out to restaurants with colleagues or customers, Bob might find that drinking (and perhaps even heavy drinking) is the norm. Under some circumstances (e.g., with customers) Bob would have to deal with the situation via newly acquired social skills of appropriately refusing a drink. On many days, however, he might plan incompatible activities, such as having lunch brought into his office, going to a restaurant that does not serve alcoholic beverages, or going home for lunch.

Situational cues are often extensive and varied, mainly because of past associations between environmental stimuli and abusive drinking. Some obvious stimuli would include those mentioned in Chapter 1—seeing alcohol advertisements, passing by a bar, observing others drinking, hearing verbal references to drinking. However, nonalcohol-related stimuli might also become associated with drinking. If an individual drinks frequently while watching television, then television watching can become a cue for drinking behavior. The goal of self-management is to narrow the range of cues that are associated with drinking. Let's examine the case of a young heavy drinker who is trying to cut down on his drinking. Let's suppose that he drinks beer in a wide variety of situations—both alone and with others, in his living room or den, in bars, watching television or reading. Each of these situational cues could potentially set off drinking behavior. His self-management program might include a plan which limits his drinking to highly specific situations. For example, he would drink only at parties, in certain bars, or with certain friends or relatives who did not drink heavily. He would never drink in any other location (e.g., in a car, at work).

A more chronic alcoholic may initially have to avoid as many of these cues (especially the more potent ones) as possible. This might require drastically changing her daily routine. For a number of weeks the client would be requested to plan an alternative schedule of activities which differs greatly from her past schedule. This also may involve rearranging activities to avoid situations. Eventually, the client can be phased back into exposure to these cues. In this way the cues become reassociated with *nondrinking* activities. If she normally has three or four drinks before dinner, the meal might be served immediately after work. After a while, dinner might be postponed for 20 minutes. During this time the client could engage in other incompatible activities, such as coffee drinking or jogging. This time could then be expanded to an hour as these new associations become established. This process of reassociation is necessary because routines are seldom 100 percent assured and the client must be flexible enough to cope with life as it really is.

## Rearranging Behavioral Consequences

In addition to rearranging precipitating cues, the client must learn to modify the *consequences* of drinking. Social environmental consequences can be very important in maintaining a pattern of excessive drinking. Immediate, as opposed to long-term, consequences most influence behavior. We are assuming that excessive drinking has led to positive immediate consequences (e.g., relaxation, ability to be more socially spontaneous) while abstinence or moderate drinking has been associated with either neutral or negative immediate consequences. This patterning of consequences typically locks an individual into a specific way of responding (i.e., chronic heavy drinking). The goal of self-management is for the client to rearrange such consequences so that she rewards herself for sobriety and punishes herself for excessive drinking.

The client and counselor must determine which activities are pleasurable for the client so that they can serve as rewards. The term **reward** or **reinforcer** as used in a more precise sense refers to any consequent event which increases the likelihood that a particular behavior will recur. Thus, the consequence would not necessarily be positive at face value. Lectures and nagging from friends subsequent to one or two drinks might consistently lead to *more* drinks by an alcoholic. Although this consequence is not a positive event, it is a reinforcer or reward as just defined. For purposes of this chapter we will be discussing rewards as positive or satisfying events. The ultimate test of consequences as rewards, however, lies in their effectiveness in modifying behavior.

The client can simply be requested to write down all of the possible activities that she finds pleasurable or satisfying. These might also include activities which, at face value, are not rated as highly pleasurable but which occur very frequently. These might include smoking, talking on the telephone, watching television, or reading. Such activities can be used also as rewards for new behavior. The client's list should include a number of activities that she can readily rearrange by *herself*. For example, planning to refrain from television watching for an evening would be an easy punishment to arrange, but refraining from all social interaction with other family members may not be. This latter maneuver would involve the cooperation and agreement of other family members, which might be difficult to obtain and/or sustain over a considerable period of time.

Once the list is complete, the client can arrange to schedule one or two of these activities (rewards) so that they occur *only* if she has remained abstinent from alcohol for a specified period. She might agree to watch television or to read in the evening only if she has refrained from alcoholic beverages for the entire day. Conversely, withholding the activity contingent upon drinking serves as a punishment for that behavior (drinking).

Public acknowledgement by the client of her intention to place consequences on her behavior in this manner helps to insure that she will implement her promises. A public statement (preferably written) to her family, friends, or employer often provides enough social pressure for the client to follow through on her self-management plan.

The case of Mary B. will be presented as an example of consequating behavior. Mary, a 21-year-old, rather outgoing, single college student, has been drinking heavily for about a year. She becomes intoxicated about three times a week and drinks daily. At the request of her counselor she lists the following activities which are pleasurable to her: dating, going to a movie or out to eat with girlfriends, going to the Student Union to see her friends, reading mystery novels, and listening to the radio. As a self-management plan, Mary agrees to the following:

1. I agree to record my drinking behavior (i.e., time of day, type of drink, number of drinks, circumstances surrounding drinking episodes) each day on an index card and to give the card to my counselor at each weekly session. For each day that I record my drinking and/or urges to drink I will allow myself to read a mystery novel or watch television for one hour that evening. If I forget to self-monitor or fail to do it accurately, I will *not* allow myself to engage in these activities.

2. I agree to try to refrain from all alcoholic beverages for the next month. For each day that I do not drink any alcoholic beverages, I will allow myself to leave my dormitory room that evening to go out to supper with a friend or go to the Student Union. For each day that I drink alcohol, I will not allow myself to leave the dorm. If I drink in the evening, I will restrict myself from the activities on the following evening. For each five-day period that I do not drink, I will allow myself to date my boyfriend. If I do drink, I will not allow myself to date for a five-day period.

The client can also arrange consequences through the assistance of others. Bill W. has been drinking heavily for 10 years and has lost numerous jobs because of his drinking. Even though Bill was a good worker when he was sober, his last employer dismissed him because drinking was interfering with his work performance. Bill has been sober for three months and asks his boss for his previous job. To help maintain control over his drinking behavior and to reassure his boss that he has given up drinking, Bill negotiates a self-management agreement with his boss. The behavior that Bill wishes to maintain is his taking Antabuse every day. He arranges to ingest Antabuse in the presence of his employer every morning when he comes to work. As a consequence of this behavior, the boss agrees to allow Bill to work that day. If Bill fails to take the Antabuse tablet for any reason, he requests that his employer not allow him to work that day. Consequences are in effect on a day-to-day basis. Bill might also arrange for his boss to provide salary increases contingent upon certain periods during which he takes Antabuse every day.

## Rearranging Cues And Consequences
## Through Cognitive Events

In addition to rearranging *external* cues and consequences, clients can also be taught to rearrange *internal* or cognitive events (i.e., what someone says to himself) for purposes of self-management. These events are usually rearranged to modify other thoughts which precipitate drinking. There are usually three types:

1. Alcohol-related thoughts (e.g., images of bars or alcoholic beverages).
2. Thoughts related to expected positive consequences of drinking (e.g., "One drink won't hurt me," "I'll be more sociable if I take a drink").
3. Nonalcohol thoughts which are functionally related to drinking behavior (e.g., "Why should I have all of these responsibilities?" "Nobody really cares about me").

*Alcohol-related thoughts.* The first category of thoughts can be modified through covert sensitization. Basically, this is a means of suppressing alcohol-related thoughts which might eventually lead to drinking. In this procedure, the client is requested to list events or experiences that are personally very unpleasant or aversive. They are usually such events as experiencing nausea and vomiting, personal ridicule, or injury in an automobile accident. The Fear Inventory described by Dr. Joseph Wolpe[1] provides a list of potentially unpleasant items which are helpful in this regard. It also is helpful to use situations the client has actually experienced. Negative situations which have occurred as a result of past drinking episodes or situations in which the client is fearful also can be used. These might include being arrested, being mugged while intoxicated, or injuring a child or relative in an automobile accident after drinking.

After these situations are accumulated, the client is requested to list all the possible visual, auditory, verbal, and tactile cognitive images that serve as cues for his abusive drinking. The object of covert sensitization is to repeatedly associate these alcohol cues with unpleasant experiences and images. To accomplish this, the client is seated in a relaxed position. While some behavioral counselors induce muscular relaxation at this time, it does not appear to be necessary. The client is requested to vividly imagine a drinking scene which the counselor describes:

"You are driving your car down the street and look from side to side. All of a sudden you see a bar with a large sign that reads "BEER." You are really thirsty and can picture a nice cold glass of beer. You really want that beer. You begin to pull into the parking lot of the bar. You see the "BEER" sign very clearly and can picture that beer. You can almost taste it going down your throat. As you continue to think about these things, you begin to have a queasy feeling in the pit of your stomach. You are feeling very sick. Your stomach is churning around and around. Your head is swimming. You feel vomit coming up into your throat. Your stomach is tied up in knots. You look up and see the "BEER" sign, and vomit comes into your mouth."

These associations are repeated over and over with emphasis placed on the client's vividly experiencing in imagination what is being described to him. The number of associations varies, but usually from 5 to 10 are included in each session for 4 to 5 sessions. The client is then instructed to practice these associations during the week. In addition, he is encouraged to bring these negative images to mind whenever he is confronted with alcohol-related cues (either cognitively or through visual or auditory senses).

*Aversion therapy—a form of self-control?* The preceding treatment is an example of covert conditioning which actually is a form of aversion therapy. Aversion therapy has been a widely used procedure in alcoholism treatment. In fact, aversion therapy with alcoholics was first reported by clinicians in the Soviet Union in 1928. Although this form of treatment is rapidly losing popularity in the United States, it remains one of the major therapeutic modalities for alcoholism in the USSR. (Treatment in Russia is often mandatory for known alcoholics. They may spend up to two years in government treatment centers.)

**Aversion therapy** consists of the repeated association of the sight, smell, taste, and thought of alcohol with unpleasant or noxious events. These events can be electrical (e.g., a painful electric shock to the arm, hand, or leg), chemical (e.g., nausea and vomiting induced by an emetic drug), or verbal as just described. These associations are repeated until the client develops a dislike for alcohol. Chemical and electrical aversion therapy are dropping out of favor of late, for several good reasons: (1) they are often very unpleasant for the client to endure, and (2) more importantly, recent treatment evaluation studies do not strongly support their effectiveness. Certainly, there have been a number of clinical successes with these techniques. However, it appears that these successes are due primarily to factors other than conditioning. For example, it is rare that clients receive aversion therapy and nothing else. Clients usually obtain advice and counseling along with it. Other therapeutic factors, such as the client's expectations or attention-placebo factors, also are extremely important in therapeutic success, even though they are often overlooked.

Aversion therapy may be more successful when it is presented to the client as a self-control device. That is, the client is not told that he is being conditioned to automatically respond negatively to alcohol cues. This statement could not, in fact, be true. Conditioning in alcoholism treatment *must* be a process which involves the active cooperation and participation of the client. The *Clockwork Orange* version of aversion therapy is simply a myth.

Dr. Albert Bandura of Stanford University also describes aversion therapy as a self-control procedure.[2] He believes that clients who are successful as a result of this technique consciously re-experience the unpleasant feelings that occurred during the aversion therapy sessions whenever they are confronted with alcohol cues or urges that are likely to elicit drinking. From this perspective, verbal aversion or covert conditioning would best provide the client with the tools for accomplishing the present goal.

*Thoughts related to the positive consequences of drinking.* The next type of cue involves thoughts about the positive consequences of drinking. In a sense, this is the process by which the alcoholic talks himself into taking a drink. The client may say, "I really didn't want that drink, but I started to argue with myself over taking it or not. I figured that a few drinks would relax me, but instead they made me more depressed. Then, I felt guilty about taking the drink in the first place."

Typically, the client does not think about the unpleasant consequences of drinking until after the drinking episode. This is true partly because the *immediate* effects of alcohol are pleasurable. Negative consequences occur later, either after a few drinks, the next day, or after many years of excessive drinking (e.g., in the case of medical complications). In the time interval immediately before the individual takes a drink, he is most probably imagining some positive consequence of drinking. He may feel that he will be more sociable, likable, relaxed, sexy, or carefree. Any thoughts of negative consequences (e.g., hangover) are overshadowed by the positive ones. To help control these precipitants of drinking, the client must be prepared. He must develop a list of potential consequences of both drinking and sobriety which will actively compete with other thoughts and eventually outweigh them.

The client and counselor together can devise a list composed of (1) potential aversive and unpleasant consequences of alcohol abuse and (2) potential positive consequences of sobriety. This list should include both short-term and long-term consequences most relevant and meaningful to the client. An example list is presented in Table 15,[3] which follows.

---

TABLE 15.    CONSEQUENCES OF BEHAVIOR
             AS SELF-CONTROL TECHNIQUES*

| Aversive Consequences of Alcohol Abuse | Positive Consequences for Abstinence or Moderate Drinking |
|---|---|
| 1. Loss of spouse and children | 1. More satisfying family life |
| 2. Loss of employment | 2. Children and spouse proud |
| 3. Loss of friends | 3. Possible promotion at work |
| 4. Cirrhosis of liver | 4. Good health; feeling well physically |
| 5. Confinement in State Hospital | 5. Recognition and approval of others |
| 6. Death due to automobile accident while intoxicated | 6. Feelings of accomplishment |
| 7. Causing the death of another while driving in an intoxicated state | |

*Reprinted with permission from P. M. Miller. *Behavioral treatment of alcoholism.* New York: Pergamon Press, 1976.

---

The next step is to assist the client to think more frequently about the consequences of drinking and sobriety. One method of accomplishing this is to associate these thoughts with other activities. In essence, activities that the client frequently engages in are used as cues for thinking about these consequences. These thoughts, then, are considered to be a new response which the client must learn. Simply telling her to think about these thoughts more often is likely to change her behavior for only a very short time. She is likely to forget to do it or to be too busy with other thoughts or activities.

Cigarette smoking, coffee drinking, or talking on the telephone are activities most people engage in frequently during the day. The client can be instructed to write the consequences on an index card and carry this card with her cigarette package. She is instructed to read each consequence on her list and think about each very vividly prior to lighting a cigarette. She may then light up and smoke the cigarette. She is to repeat this sequence prior to each cigarette during the day. This procedure insures that the client will think about the consequences on her list often during the day and also serves to reward thinking about these events with a pleasurable activity.

Certainly the counselor would not want the client to spend every day of her life thinking about the consequences of her drinking behavior. The above procedure should, however, be continued for approximately two to three weeks. Then the counselor can begin to narrow down the situations in which these new thought patterns occur. After this period, the client is instructed to read and think about her list only when cues related to drinking behavior are present. For example, she might hear some friends discussing having a drink after work. This may lead to thoughts of "I'd really like to have just one myself. I'm sure they wouldn't let me overdo it." Immediately upon hearing her friends' conversation, she should examine her list of consequences and vividly think about them.

It is important that the client imagine these consequences in detail and try to experience them in her imagination. That is, she might imagine the feelings involved in causing the death of another while intoxicated or the positive feelings of being awarded a promotion because of her work performance and sobriety. The client should be encouraged to utilize all of her imaginative senses in this regard so that she sees, hears, and feels the experience. This method provides more potency to these thoughts, enabling them to override other intrusive thoughts about potential positive effects of alcohol.

*Nonalcohol-related thoughts.* In many cases, the alcoholic's drinking is precipitated by thoughts that are not directly related to alcohol *per se.* These thoughts might be self-derogatory, guilt-related, retaliatory, or involve "getting away from it all." These cues can be approached from two directions. First, the counselor must examine the social-emotional events associated with these thoughts. For example, what specific interpersonal conflicts result in self-derogatory or retaliatory thoughts. Once these are identified, the client must be taught alternative ways to successfully cope with them. Methods of teaching these interpersonal and problem-solving skills are described elsewhere (see Chapters 4, 5, 6, 7, 9). Second, the counselor can teach the client to either question the logic of the thought patterns that he is having and/or to replace them with competing thoughts. For example, Dr. Albert Ellis has developed a system of rational-emotive therapy based on these goals.[4] Clients are taught to analyze and question the sequence of their thought patterns. The assumption is that individuals often make illogical assumptions about situations based on emotional rather than rational thinking and that it is these assumptions which lead to psychological distress. The client is instructed to pay attention to "the statements that you are making to yourself!" An example follows.

Richard E. is a 33-year-old problem drinker whose alcohol consumption is often precipitated by thoughts regarding his own worthlessness. Richard has been completely abstinent from all alcoholic beverages for three months and is beginning to feel better about himself. One day at work, Richard's boss berates him for a mistake that he has made. The boss is very angry with Richard. Richard is very upset by this incident, and as he drives home that evening he begins to think more about it. His sequence of statements to himself continue as follows:

1. "I really made a terrible mistake."
2. "I must be stupid for doing such a thing."
3. "I'm just no damned good."
4. "My boss was sure sore at me."
5. "He probably doesn't like me any more because he was so angry and I'm so dumb."
6. "I guess nobody really cares about me because I'm not worth caring about."

Richard has made a number of jumps in rational logic in this sequence. He assumes that because he made a mistake, he is not very intelligent and is completely worthless. He also assumes that since his boss became angry with him, neither his boss nor anybody else cares about him. The counselor's objective is to encourage the client to (1) more objectively evaluate the situation in question and (2) question the validity of each statement he makes to himself. For example, Richard might begin by questioning whether he was, in fact, responsible for the mistake. Some individuals tend to blame themselves for everything that goes wrong. Others, of course, refuse to accept responsibility for any of their behavior and try to blame others for their own deficiencies. In either case, the client must more objectively evaluate the mistake. Was the boss justified in blaming Richard? If so, Richard must accept the responsibility and learn to deal with it. If not, perhaps Richard should be taught more effective ways of sticking up for his rights with his boss.

Let's suppose that, in this case, Richard was to blame. Thus, his first statement to himself ("I really made a terrible mistake") is true and logical. His second statement based on this first one is *not* logical. That is, he is definitely *not* stupid because he made one mistake. Richard must learn to immediately question this assumption and practice saying more logical and perhaps more positive statements such as, "Well, I've learned to be more careful the next time" or "I'll have to remember to double check that the next time." There is a crucial difference between a person who says, "I am stupid" and one who says, "I have acted in a stupid way." A basically intelligent person may, at times, act in stupid ways, and a basically successful person will, at times, meet with failure.

Richard's next assumption, "I'm just no damned good," is even more illogical. Richard must learn to base his worth as an individual not on transient situational factors but on more stable behavioral characteristics (e.g., "I'm a kind and generous person"). Making a mistake is not in any way related to these stable characteristics and, therefore, cannot change them.

Statement No. 4 appears to be correct, but the assumptions that follow it are not. In his next two statements (No. 5 and No. 6) Richard assumes that since his boss is angry with him, he also dislikes him and perhaps even hates him. In addition, since his boss dislikes him, everyone else must dislike him. Richard must learn to avoid such generalizations and at least try out alternative statements to himself. For example, he must learn that being angry with someone is usually a short-lived phenomenon and does not necessarily indicate hatred.

In addition to self-questioning from a logical point of view, clients can also be taught to practice making statements to themselves that are more positive or goal directed. Many alcoholics tend to emphasize their negative characteristics. If an individual constantly tells himself that he is no good or unable to do anything well, his behavior will be negatively affected. In a sense, we are what we tell ourselves. Positive self-reference thoughts can be increased in much the same way that we discussed increasing thoughts about the consequences of drinking behaviors. That is, clients can list on an index card a number of positive qualities about themselves. Most clients will need assistance in doing this since they are just not accustomed to thinking about themselves in a positive way. Reading and thinking about this list can then be rewarded with pleasurable activities or the opportunity to engage in a frequently occurring behavior (e.g., drinking coffee).

## MAINTAINING SELF-CONTROL SKILLS

### The Counselor's Attitude

After the counselor has taught the client self-management skills and the two have agreed on a self-management strategy to use, how does the counselor insure that the client will continue to use these skills? The first rule of thumb is to realize that self-management behaviors are new for the individual and not part of her routine. These are behaviors that must be modified, i.e., increased, just as the client's other behaviors must be modified, e.g., drinking. Counselors frequently become disenchanted and angry when clients do not comply with their instructions. That is, the counselor may claim that a client who has failed to monitor her drinking urges over the past week is "unmotivated" or "being spiteful for not doing what I tell her." It is almost as if the counselor is saying "She doesn't appreciate what I'm doing for her." The major point is that if the client could readily self-manage her behavior with minimal instructions, she would hardly need a trained counselor! All she would need is a how-to-do it book on self-control! The counselor, however, must evaluate the client's difficulty in self-managing in terms of what she, the counselor, is doing (or not doing) rather than in terms of the motivation of the client. The counselor should not be saying, "What is wrong with the client? Why isn't she taking my advice?" The counselor should be asking, "What must I do to increase the likelihood that the client will engage in self-management behaviors?"

### Using Cues

To do this, the counselor must determine what factors are hindering the client from completing assigned tasks. One method of determining the general problems involved in self-management is for the counselor to use this procedure on her own behavior. It will readily become apparent that self-management is not as easy as it appears. Clients often say that they forgot to monitor their behavior or that they were doing other things. Frequently, clients must be given a cue to help them remember to self-manage. A readily available visual cue is useful. When self-monitoring is the desired response, an index card or a graph can be kept in locations where the behavior being monitored is likely to occur. The individual will be reminded to self-monitor when he sees that particular cue.

### Appropriate Scheduling Of Strategies

It must also be remembered that self-management procedures often disrupt an individual's life. A client is not likely to engage in these activities if they disrupt important or pleasurable aspects of his life or if they are scheduled to occur when other, competing, events are also occurring. An individual is not likely to read or think about a list of negative consequences of drinking if, at the same time, he is at a business meeting or social gathering. The counselor must identify the circumstances in which self-management occurs and determine factors which are competing with this new behavior. She might then arrange for self-management strategies to be implemented only at specified times.

### Pacing Practice

Some clients, especially those who are having the most difficulty in implementing self-management skills, must begin at a slower pace. Less must be expected of them at first. For example, a client who is unable to practice a self-management procedure three times a day may be able to do it once a day. At first, he may be asked only to engage in the behavior two or three times per week. When that pattern becomes established, a new criterion of performance is set up mutually by the counselor and client.

### Using Behavioral Contracts

Behavioral contracts are often helpful to sustain self-management behaviors. These contracts are written agreements between the client and counselor in which behavioral consequences are prearranged.

John W. has decided to rearrange the consequences of his drinking. He sets aside $100 in a special checking account and decides that whenever he has an alcoholic beverage, he must write a check on this account for $20 to one of his most disliked political organizations. About a month later, John has three drinks on his way home from work. The next day, he thinks about his agreement with himself. Although he knows that he should write the check, he says, "Oh well, I've learned my lesson. And besides, I can't afford to lose that much money." Thus, John fails to self-manage his behavior.

John and his counselor discuss this problem and decide to negotiate a contract with one another. John opens a joint account with the counselor and deposits $250 into it. The two devise a written contract which authorizes the counselor to write a $50 check to John's most disfavored political organization if John drinks alcohol (as determined by either John's self-report, John's wife's report, or the counselor's observations of John's behavior). In this way, John has self-managed his behavior by arranging specified behavioral consequences to occur through the intervention of others.

Some clients find it useful to write a contract with themselves. They might write up a formal agreement such as:

I, Robert M., promise to watch television and/or work on my woodworking hobby *only* if I have read and thought about my list of drinking consequences three times during the day. These times must have occurred once in the morning, once in the afternoon, and once in the evening. If I fail to read and think about this list on any occasion, I will not watch television or work on my hobby that evening.

---

Robert M.

Robert can post this agreement in a conspicuous place in his household to make public his agreement with himself. This places additional social pressure on him to abide by the agreement and helps to remind him of his promises. This particular agreement demonstrates one other factor in self-management. Robert is actually using one self-management behavior (rearranging consequences) to modify another self-management behavior (thinking of certain cognitive events).

## Rewarding Positive Behavior

Rewarding consequences must be applied to self-management behaviors to insure their stability over time. For example, a client might be requested to monitor his drinking behavior. Let's suppose that he reports to his counselor that he had four drinks the previous week and, as he was instructed, wrote down the number of drinks, circumstances, etc. In the early stages of intervention, the counselor should reward or pay attention to the *self-monitoring behavior* rather than the drinking behavior. Focusing on the negative aspects of drinking or on the importance of complete abstinence may punish the client for accurate self-monitoring and thus punish him for telling the counselor the truth. In fact, the deceptiveness of an alcoholic regarding his drinking is practically a cliche character description. Could it be, however, that relatives, friends, and counselors teach the alcoholic to be deceptive through their responses to his accurate reports of drinking? In fact, significant others often respond to the alcoholic's having one drink in as negative a way as they respond to his having 20 drinks. The alcoholic's success at having just one drink and then stopping usually goes unnoticed. Alcoholics often use this reaction as a reason to continue drinking once it has begun by thinking, "I'll catch hell whether I have one drink or ten so I might as well have the ten."

## ADVANTAGES OF TEACHING SELF-MANAGEMENT SKILLS

Several advantages accrue from teaching clients self-management skills. First, they become active participants in the therapeutic process. They, in a sense, are learning to become their own counselors. They are learning to assess and modify their own behavior. This active involvement together with the weekly homework assignments provided to clients enable the counselor to more readily assess motivation to change. More importantly, it allows the counselor to define motivation behaviorally in terms of which assignments the client is not carrying out.

Second, changing behavior patterns via self-management frequently is accompanied by feelings of increased self-esteem and self-worth. The client feels a sense of accomplishment at changing her own behavior.

Third, self-management training provides a method of analyzing behavior which is not merely relevant to the client's specific problems at the time of counseling. It provides her with a *response set* for evaluating personal problems and then planning and implementing a therapeutic plan on her own. The benefits of counseling generalize to a wide variety of present and future problem areas.

*Footnotes*

1. J. Wolpe. *The practice of behavior therapy.* New York: Pergamon Press, Inc., 1973.

2. A. Bandura. *Principles of behavior modification.* New York: Holt, Rinehart, and Winston, Inc., 1969.

3. P. M. Miller. *Behavioral treatment of alcoholism.* New York: Pergamon Press, Inc., 1976.

4. A. Ellis. *Reason and emotion in psychotherapy.* New York: Lyle-Stuart, 1962.

# 9 Occupational Skills Training

## SIGNIFICANCE OF JOB

In a society that ranks its citizens according to their productivity, a person without employment is placed in a very low position unless there is an acceptable, discernible reason for this lack. Alcoholism is not one of the acceptable reasons. Yet there are few disorders that can cause such disruption to one's life and especially to one's work. Statistically, alcoholism has caused a greater waste of industrial time, money, and human potential than any other disorder. The recent support of prevention and early detection provided by business is one indication of the magnitude of the problem.

Counselors who work with alcoholic individuals indicate that often the job is the last to go in the long list of losses the individual experiences. The significance of job loss to the individual's self-image cannot be overestimated. Most adults rely on their jobs not only to ensure them financial stability but also for friends, social contacts, parties, etc. The employer and co-workers are in control of a wide range of rewards and punishers. The person out of work does not have this rich resource and usually has difficulty meeting these needs in other ways.

Part of the rehabilitation of the alcoholic is the restructuring of her life. This general restructuring entails physical, social, psychological, and financial rehabilitation. The vocational area ideally demonstrates the interaction of these areas. The decision to re-enter a situation as powerful as the one described may be difficult. In this chapter we will offer suggestions and plans to help the alcoholic individual obtain employment and cope with the stress of the job.

## THE ROLE OF THE COUNSELOR IN VOCATIONAL REHABILITATION

Little has been written to guide the counselor in the task of vocational rehabilitation of the alcoholic. In fact, there are still many who feel it is inappropriate to expect an alcoholism counselor to deal with these problems. Nevertheless, the counselor who does attempt to work with clients in obtaining employment will realize that unless this is offered, a treatment program remains incomplete. Later, when we discuss the role of employment in maintenance treatment, this will be more evident.

In dealing with vocational rehabilitation, the counselor must attend to certain clearly defined areas. These areas include: (1) job readiness of the client; (2) assessment of marketable skills; (3) availability of job opportunities; (4) knowledge of steps necessary in looking for employment; (5) on-job counseling and follow-up.

The counselor should expect to take an active role in preparing a client for employment. Most of the techniques described in this chapter may be used with individuals or with groups. We suggest that the support and help clients give each other in groups recommends this mode of treatment. Clients who are prone to think "Why me?" or "No one else has this problem" benefit substantially when they share a common problem with others.

## JOB READINESS

Just as the alcoholic's job is usually the last thing lost, so often it is the first goal sought in her attempt to recover. The counselor may sometimes have to make a distinction between job readiness and "job willingness," for a client's wish to be employed may not equal her capability to maintain a job successfully. One just recovering from the physical and emotional deterioration of alcoholism would have little to offer an employer and would gain just as little by the experience.

So, an initial assessment must be made by the counselor to determine the client's readiness to work. A group composed of men and women also desirous of employment is a beneficial and efficient manner in which to make this assessment. The following excerpt from such a group will illustrate this:

> Joe: I haven't worked for years. I don't think I'd even know how to *look* for a job.
>
> Jean: Anybody can get a job. All you have to do is pound the pavement.
>
> Mary: What about your problem? Anybody can tell you're an alcoholic! What are you going to tell them?
>
> Jean: It's nobody's business!

146

It is obvious that Jean would have a very hard time getting a job, and, in fact, job-hunting at this point may be a negative experience in itself.

Mary, another client, brought up one of the essential questions in job counseling. This particular question is one on which counselors should expect to spend several sessions. We will deal with it in detail in a later section of the chapter. The point to be made here concerns the group's function: questions such as this one usually have more impact when a group member states them. Other areas that might be included for discussion in such a group include expectations, fears, and questions which the client has about obtaining employment. Table 16 may be used to stimulate the group's thinking.

---

TABLE 16.    GUIDE FOR COUNSELORS
IN PREPARING CLIENTS FOR WORK:
TYPICAL CLIENT REACTIONS

*Expectations*

1. Once I have a job, my family will come back to me.

2. If my boss and co-workers knew I had a drinking problem, they would treat me differently.

3. A job would give me a sure way of meeting my needs of belonging, accomplishment, acceptance, etc.

*Fears*

1. I may fall short, be inadequate, begin to drink again under the pressure of the job.

*Questions*

1. How do I handle questions about my absences, unemployment periods?

2. What do I say when everyone orders drinks at lunch?

3. What do I do when I feel the urge to drink on the job?

---

In the example, the counselor, seeing Jean's defensiveness and choosing to move the focus off her, may take the opportunity to follow through by asking the group what indeed they would tell a prospective employer about their drinking problem. Keeping in mind the purpose of the group, the assessment of job readiness, and preparation for more specific skills training, the counselor would attempt to desensitize the members to handling the question.

In Jean's case, the counselor decides that she is not ready to actively seek employment but must work on certain defensive attitudes that cause her to cut off discussion of pertinent topics.

Joe, on the other hand, expressed uncertainty and a need to learn *how* to look for a job. By stating his need he seemed responsive to learning and would probably benefit from the more structured steps involved in vocational rehabilitation.

## ASSESSMENT OF MARKETABLE SKILLS

Clients who have been unemployed for years may lack marketable skills. The vocational rehabilitation group at Beth Israel Medical Center, in New York[1] suspect, however, that because of our inexperience in vocational work, we are too quick to relegate a client to an unemployable status and to resolve the problem by recommending welfare support, sheltered workshop, or a menial job. Their survey showed a clientele which possessed a large variety of interests and skills, non-functional but readily amenable to vocational training and on-the-job development.

Naturally, a skill is less available the longer it is unused and the more specialized it is. This may be especially disconcerting to the person who has lost such everyday abilities as recent or remote memory, visual acuity, and hand steadiness. The alcoholic frequently must face these types of loss. Realistically evaluating the skills and abilities that are permanently lost, those that can be recovered by retraining, and those that are intact is the first step in the restoration of job skills.

Parts of this assessment are obviously out of the counselor's area of competence. A consultation or a referral to an agency, such as Vocational Rehabilitation, is appropriate if the potential worker herself cannot accomplish the evaluation/rehabilitation of necessary work skills. Generally, the evaluation should cover areas specific to the type of employment the client will be seeking. These areas include: (1) knowledge necessary to carry out the particular job; (2) abilities to carry out the tasks; (3) personal appearance; (4) necessary social skills.

## AVAILABILITY OF JOB OPPORTUNITIES

Availability of job opportunities is limited by the client's drinking problem, her spotty work record, insufficient skills, prejudices concerning the hiring of alcoholic workers, legal barring of alcoholics from certain employment, and general unavailability of jobs, especially in high-

148

density urban areas. These limitations should be kept in mind so that a client is not given false hope.

Most alcoholism counselors now realize the need to keep abreast of potential job possibilities and even to actively seek openings for their clients. In addition, industry is becoming more receptive to hiring recovered alcoholics, especially those in follow-up treatment.

Many companies are actively involved in alcoholism treatment programs designed to detect early signs of problem drinking. Their offer to alcoholic workers is simple—continuing on the job in return for their involvement in treatment. Counselors have labeled this "constructive coercion." These programs have been successful in the early detection and checking of alcoholism, and they also have helped weaken the prejudices associated with the hiring of alcoholic people. Table 17, derived from work by Dr. R. Farber,[2] lists early symptoms which employers look for in detecting drinking problems.

## STEPS TO EMPLOYMENT

### Need For Checking And Guidelines
In working with people who have been out of employment for an extended period of time, one soon realizes that the initial steps of seeking employment are frequently the most difficult for them. The counselor sees individuals who want jobs but tell no one of their desire or fail to inquire with the Personnel Departments of local businesses. Too, they may fail to evaluate the appropriateness of the work. For example, John came back to the alcoholism rehabilitation center to report he had finally gotten a job as a bartender! The question of setting himself up to fail was brought up in his therapy group. A lively discussion between him and the other members of the group concluded with this client admitting he was putting himself in an untenable position. He decided another type of work would be more appropriate.

These are the kinds of situations that make evident the need for guidelines in seeking and evaluating work situations. The sophistication of the client indicates the type of guidelines needed. Some clients may never have held jobs and would need to obtain Social Security cards. Certain groups, such as adolescents and women who have not worked outside the home, are especially in need of intensive guidance during the preliminary steps of employment seeking. Table 18 lists steps taken in finding available jobs. This chart may be used in several ways: as a tool to assess the client's skill, as a checklist for the client to follow, and as a guide to teach a client how to find available jobs.

We have found that counselors are apt to presume that the client

## TABLE 17.    SYMPTOMS OF ON-THE-JOB DRINKING*

1. *Chronic Absenteeism*—One of the chief motivators to the development of alcoholism programs by industry is the loss of half or full days, especially after weekends or holidays.

2. *Absences from work station*—The frequency of work station absences increase in order to hide from others, calm down, or have a drink.

3. *Uneven work pace*—In an effort to avoid accidents, the worker may deliberately slow down while under the influence of alcohol.

4. *Lowered quantity and quality of work*—This is especially evident after lunchtime drinking.

5. *Avoidance of supervisors or co-workers*—The worker may avoid others who might detect on-the-job drinking or other symptoms.

6. *Change in behavior*—A social person may become an isolate, a moody individual may become outgoing, especially after lunchtime drinking.

7. *Physical signs*—Most readily apparent are hand tremors, chronic hangovers, red or bleary eyes, flushed face.

8. *Lying*—The worker may begin by fabricating excuses for absences and continue until all aspects of his/her deterioration are covered in this manner.

9. *Increase in accidents*—This is especially evident when machinery is used.

*Adapted with permission from publisher. R. Farber. *Handbook for the alcoholism counselor.* Baltimore: Alcoholism Center, Baltimore City Health Department, 1970.

---

possesses a skill. We advise routine assessment since basic skills are often found lacking and may cause the client the greatest problems. The case of Lee will clearly explain this.

At the end of the first session of a work group, the counselor assigned the participants the task of circling three jobs in the classified ads of the evening newspaper.

Everyone, except Lee, came prepared to the next session. Lee, who lived in a rural area of the state, had never needed to use that section of the newspaper so, naturally, the format as well as the abbreviations were beyond his capability. A quick check and demonstration by the counselor would have eliminated a source of frustration for Lee.

---

TABLE 18.    WAYS TO FIND JOBS THAT ARE AVAILABLE

1. Read the classified section of the local newspaper.
2. Place an ad of availability in the newspaper, on appropriate bulletin boards, and in trade papers.
3. Telephone local personnel officers or employers in the field(s) that are appropriate; for example, a teacher should call the Board of Education in each city within traveling distance as well as officers of individual private schools.
4. Tell friends, family, and acquaintances that you are seeking employment and request they let you know of "leads."

---

Another equally important skill which should not be assumed to exist is that of telephoning to inquire about job availability or to answer an ad or make an interview appointment. Structured practice in telephone use is effective. This can be done by breaking the group into triads and assigning each participant to act out a part. Each participant, in turn, acts out the employer, the potential employee, and the critic (a most necessary part of this practice). The critic watches and listens to the other two actors, and when they finish, she tells each the positive and negative aspects of his or her acting, emphasizing, of course, the verbal communication.

The purpose of this task is to teach the client: (1) how to introduce herself over the telephone and state her request; (2) how to field questions and requirements, such as "briefly describe work experiences" and give personal data; (3) when and how to ask for a personal interview; (4) how to terminate the conversation.

### The Application

The employment application gives the potential employee an opportunity to fully and thoughtfully present personal data, emphasize experience and attributes, and explain employment interruptions, police records, and job dismissals. *The application also provides a preview to the interview* since many employers and personnel directors use this as a guide. Most applications are similar, and the potential employee should be encouraged to fill out a sample to help her in the oftentimes redundant business of application writing.

In this section we will describe certain areas of the application and problems arising from it and will offer suggestions which may help the client present a positive picture to the employer.

*Assets.* How the applicant highlights her assets is especially important to the alcoholic just returning to work. In reporting *skills,* the applicant should focus on those necessary to the work for which she is applying. A brief description of how the skill has been used is more impressive than merely listing it. Likewise, *previous experience* is more easily remembered by the interviewer if, in addition to the usual information on dates and duties, the applicant describes special projects or honors. An example of an entry under *Experiences* by Joe M. shows how he enhanced his assets:

12 May 1974–1 September 1974       Life guard on Ocean Beach, California

Awarded life-saving medal for saving drowning child

*"I have a drinking problem."* *If* and *how* to present the fact that one is an alcoholic has caused many to decide to delay seeking employment. We suggest that the delay simply causes additional problems. Many have decided not to report the alcoholism. In certain instances, this may be necessary. Although this is the individual's decision, the pressure to continue hiding the problem of alcohol abuse is emotionally taxing and tiring. This decision is one which warrants full discussion of advantages and disadvantages. Of course, prejudices are still strong, and the applicant may feel a job would be out of reach if the employer knew of the problem.

If one does decide to report the alcohol problem, careful thought about its presentation is needed. The application is an excellent opportunity to describe how one has been motivated to undertake full treatment for the problem and how much of what was learned in treatment is transferable to the work situation. Approaching potentially damaging situations in a constructive manner is impressive to many interviewers. For example, Jane M. described how she learned to ask for help in such a way that she and the person asked maintained their self-esteem whatever the outcome. She then described how she might use this new skill if she were offered the salesperson's position for which she was applying.

*Absenteeism and police records.* There are several other potentially harmful items on the application. One concerns the account for lost work time, both *absenteeism* and *time between employment.* The other concerns the usual inquiry about *police records.* Most people with even a rudimentary awareness of alcoholism associate these two problems with the disorder. In fact, it is an unusual situation to find an alcoholic individual who has not had difficulty with both absenteeism and the legal system. With this in mind, a brief report of information with a reminder that the individual has now taken steps to prevent further occurrence of these problems is in order. An alternative method would be to discuss this section in the personal interview, merely stating on the application the wish to discuss it in person.

*References.* The request for *references* is an excellent opportunity to allay a potential employer's fears that the applicant would be a troublesome employee. It is often advisable to list the alcoholism counselor who has helped with treatment of the drinking problem. This shows the applicant's serious intent to continue appropriate treatment and may relieve the employer of feelings that the applicant, if hired, might expect undue consideration on the job if problems, job-related or otherwise, were to arise.

## The Interview

The interview gives the client an opportunity to clarify information, emphasize strengths, and explain the alcoholism and related problems more fully.

Practice of appropriate interview behavior will give the applicant confidence to pursue "job leads." The counselor should demonstrate appropriate verbal and nonverbal behaviors in areas where the applicant has difficulty. Table 19 lists the behaviors.

---

*TABLE 19.  INTERVIEW-SKILLS TRAINING*

| *Situations* | *Procedures* |
|---|---|
| 1. *Preliminary*: Coping with pre-interview stress and anxiety. | Anxiety can be lessened to a manageable degree by being prepared fully and by specific anti-anxiety training such as the relaxation training procedure. |
| 2. Presenting oneself to the appropriate personnel, for example, secretary. | Counselor and client(s) discuss appropriate dress and verbal and nonverbal manner, practice fully stating the |

*Table 19, cont.*

3. Handling introductions.

purpose of appointment, and critique each client's practice performance.

Clients practice and critique assertive introductions attending to voice tone, full sentences, statement of name and appropriate introductory remarks, correct posture, firm handshake.

4. *Interview Proper:*
   a. Giving background information, answering open-ended questions, stating reasons why client applied for particular position, what he can offer, expects, etc.
   b. Reviewing application, filling in details, elaborating on points, discussing the drinking problem and how it is being handled, initiating discussion in areas not covered.
   c. Asking questions concerning the position, the place, working conditions, salary, benefits, etc.

Counselor demonstrations, client practice, and critique are used extensively. Audio and videotaping are excellent. The client should have the experience of several kinds of interviews including a stress interview. Interviewees often hesitate to question the interviewer for fear of being thought aggressive. On the contrary, such questions are expected and are appropriate. In fact, they are essential to the decision whether to accept a position. Again, discussion and directed practice are used.

5. *Concluding the interview:*
   a. Making final statements and clarifications.
   b. Asking for feedback.
   c. Giving feedback.

As the interview is drawing to a close, the client should quickly review the session, bringing up points not previously made. Client can learn to pick up verbal and nonverbal reactions.

6. *Terminating the interview:*
   a. Final social amenities.
   b. Asking for date by which decision will be made.

Closure is important. It is appropriate for the client to request a call or letter on the decision.

*Table 19, cont.*

| 7. *Post-interview:* | Post-interview stress is handled in the |
|---|---|
| Evaluating the interview; coping with the stress derived from the session. | same manner as preliminary stress. Both pre- and post-interview, the desire to drink for a calming effect may be present, so provisions taken to handle it are necessary. |

The following excerpt illustrates how the table is used in interview-skills training.

*George*
(Head down, playing with a loose shirt button): Yes, I have been in treatment for quite some time for my drinking and it is no longer a problem in my daily life. The treatment center and, in particular, my counselor, Jane Smith, have worked with me and I feel I've gotten a great deal out of it. I do intend to continue follow-up treatment just to be on the safe side.

*Counselor*
George, you phrased that response just right. However, I picked up feelings of embarrassment and uncertainty. I believe I was reacting to your keeping your head down and fooling with that button. Let's switch parts and see what you think.

The counselor portrays George as described above, exaggerating the problem areas slightly to make an impact on the client. Next, George practices new nonverbal behaviors until they are comfortable and feel natural.

After the first interview, he and the counselor discuss the interview and work on behaviors that need improvement. The counselor praises George for his accomplishments and efforts.

It is especially important that the counselor offer George the emotional support to withstand several refusals before obtaining an offer of employment. Both counselor and client must recognize the stress associated with seeking employment. They must realize that the client may be vulnerable to depression, to the use of alcohol, or to other maladaptive behavior. Anticipating setbacks and planning for them are necessary parts of the program. It is also necessary to plan for the client's success. For example, in the past, George used promotions or other successes as times for celebration when he would invite friends to share victory drinks. Alternative celebration tactics should be worked out.

## ACCEPTING EMPLOYMENT

Obtaining employment brings new pleasures and problems. As with the seeking of employment, the anticipation and practice of new behaviors give the employee a better chance of success.

Three areas of particular importance are: (1) assuming responsibilities; (2) work schedule; (3) interpersonal relations.

### Responsibilities

Additional responsibilities may cause a client to seek anxiety reduction through liquor. Eager to please or unsure of how to say no, clients may find themselves involved in too many tasks. In follow-up groups the new employee can be helped to anticipate such situations and develop methods of handling them. An example of how a person out of work for over a year may handle situations such as these follows: Lou is a 40-year-old journalist who has just obtained employment on the basis of her letters of recommendation and copies of unpublished work. She has had wide experience, and her previous employers always remark about her enthusiasm for all her assignments. Her new employer decided that enthusiasm is the needed element for a new project entailing about two months of travel throughout the United States. In the past, Lou has had special difficulty with her drinking when she has been away from home, so she had resolved to avoid such situations if at all possible. Faced with the problem of refusing the assignment or risking the potential danger of two months away from home, Lou accepts the assignment. At home she and her family argue about the decision. Everyone is too involved and too frightened to think rationally about the problem. Lou's counselor is consulted at this point because of the contract she, her family, and the counselor have, which outlines how they will work together. The joint meeting is designed as a problem-solving session in which the following format is used:

1. The problem is presented in a concise manner by the person who is primarily affected—in this case, Lou.
2. All other members are given an opportunity to clarify, elaborate, or add to Lou's presentation.
3. Solutions and their positive and negative aspects are offered by group members. All solutions are considered.
4. Choices are narrowed down by the group members and rediscussed.

5. A decision is made by the group, with the person who is primarily involved having a major part in the decision making.
6. Steps needed to carry out the decision are discussed.

Each problem-solving session is used not only to solve a particular problem but also to learn how to solve other problems. As the group learns problem-solving skills, the counselor is needed less until finally the group members may assume full responsibility.

In this example, Lou and her family agreed that two months away from home would not be beneficial to her. They decided she would talk with her employer, who was aware of Lou's drinking problem, and offer alternatives to the extended traveling period. The group expected the employer to be agreeable to an alternative plan but if not, the same problem-solving tactics would be used again.

There are times when the responsibilities inherent in a job may become overwhelming. When there is danger of this occurring, the counselor might suggest setting up a list of priorities. Tasks that must be completed immediately are put on the top, and those which can wait are placed lower on the list. As tasks are completed, they are checked off. In this way, one may keep track of tasks still pending and may be rewarded for tasks completed. Such lists may be prepared on a daily, weekly, or monthly basis. It is helpful to decide on reasonable time allotments for each task. Especially for those who have not been on a schedule for some time, lists help structure the day and make a job more manageable.

## Work Schedule

Consideration should be given to the new employee's work schedule. Sufficient time to finish tasks, avoidance of overloads, a balance of active and sedentary tasks, and planned coffee and lunch breaks will make for a more productive and less taxing day. Studies show that those who work according to schedule are less tired at the end of the day.

## Interpersonal Relations

The manner in which one deals with various personalities is an equally important aspect of a new job. The new employee should be able to handle disagreements in a manner which will solve the presenting problem and also leave the disagreeing members' self-esteem intact. The counselor may assess the client's ability to handle certain interpersonal situations by asking what difficult situations she has encountered in the past or by setting up typical situations which may arise and observing how the client reacts. An ideal way to assess and remedy deficiencies or excesses in interpersonal relationships is in a group composed of people in similar situations.

Groups allow the participants to share experiences and suggestions, praise one another, act out situations, and critique each other. An important by-product of such a group is the opportunity to come together with others in similar situations, realizing that one is not alone in having such problems. Groups in which members who have "graduated" and come back to share their experiences often cause others to redouble their efforts in working toward change.

An example of one such graduate is a 38-year-old male with a history of being fired from jobs. Assessment showed that Mr. M. would become angry when his supervisor directed him in the minute details of his job on a heavy machine. He would passively resist such direction by looking away or standing between the supervisor and the machine. But Mr. M. had never simply told the supervisor that he had a master rating on the machine and needed no direction. Finally, Mr. M. would have enough, berate the supervisor, and walk off the job. When Mr. M. entered the work group, his goal was to learn alternative ways of handling such situations. He first enacted the situation as it occurred. A group member who had been briefed on the supervisor's behavior played opposite Mr. M.

Mr. M. and the "supervisor" then explained how they felt during the scene. The group critiqued the role playing and offered suggestions to Mr. M. on how he could handle the situation in a constructive manner. Verbal and nonverbal communication was discussed. Mr. M. then practiced until he felt comfortable to handle the situation in real life. A six-month follow-up showed Mr. M. was on the same job—the longest time he had held a job.

## SITUATIONS THAT MAY LEAD TO DRINKING

Beginning a new job necessitates the use of a whole range of behaviors previously not required of the client. Neither the counselor nor the client should assume that the counseling relationship has been completed once the client is working. Employment merely creates a new phase to vocational counseling. Follow-up groups are ideal in handling this new phase in the client's development. Not only is the group used to express the excitement and fears inherent in new situations, but it is also used in a structured problem-solving manner. A list of appropriate topics for follow-up group work is presented in Table 20.

## TABLE 20.    FOLLOW-UP GROUP TOPICS

1. Work load and added responsibilities

2. Dealing with authority

3. Being an effective supervisor

4. Alcohol-related topics
   a. work route consists of streets with taverns or liquor stores
   b. during luncheons and business meetings alcohol is freely available
   c. the stress, loneliness, and availability of liquor associated with business travel and conventions

5. Dealing with people on the job and socially

6. The new availability of money

7. How to spend leisure time

## Travel Routes

Routes traveled to and from work may cause problems if the alcoholic must pass taverns, lounges, or liquor stores. Even the most determined person is sure to weaken when temptation is constantly put in his way. The point is not to test one's will power or make a moral issue of abstaining from alcohol but simply to abstain in the easiest ways possible. Walking or driving an additional quarter-mile may be an effective deterrent to after-work drinking. See Chapter 8 for more details on self-management.

## Business Luncheons And Meetings

Business luncheons and meetings are times when alcohol may be used to provide an atmosphere of comradeship and relaxation in days which may be high pressured. To refuse such an offer of friendship may be an assertive act beyond the client's present functioning. This client's task, then, would be to practice saying "no" assertively. (See Chapter 5 for assertion training.) Until this is accomplished, blaming physical disorders such as diabetes for the need to abstain is a useful ploy. If one uses the same restaurants frequently throughout the week, a prearrangement with the bartender to bring the "usual," a nonalcoholic drink, is also a solution.

## Travel And Conventions

Traveling and attending conventions are also areas of concern for clients. For some, the loneliness on the road with successive nights spent in hotel rooms is deadened by alcohol. Salespeople, truck drivers, and others who find that drinking is especially difficult to control while traveling might try rearranging schedules so that not more than one night at a time is spent away from home. Traveling with a companion and changing jobs are also alternatives.

Conventions often cause problems in that strangeness, loneliness, work oriented around luncheons, and bar contacts offer too many pitfalls to overcome. Careful prearrangement of schedules and attendance with a relative or sympathetic co-worker are often the best strategies when such meetings cannot be avoided.

## Schedules

After spending months, perhaps years, with no obligations, one may find realistic schedules difficult to set up. The client will need to take small steps and slowly work out time structures that meet his needs. Not only are schedules called for on the job but also off the job. As the client's time for leisure and home-oriented tasks is filled, his whole life becomes more manageable with structuring.

As previously mentioned, meeting work deadlines is more possible when bits of the task are worked into the daily schedule. Special projects may call for large blocks of time which must be planned days or weeks in advance. So, too, home maintenance tasks, such as laundry, house cleaning, and cooking, are best done on schedule. It is easy to ignore these tasks, especially if one lives alone. Maintaining a pleasant household, free from debt or overwhelming chores, provides a respite from the work day and a haven in which to spend leisure time with family and acquaintances met on the job.

## Budgeting

As structuring of time is essential to a well-balanced life so, too, is financial structuring. A budget of monthly expenses may be used to deter the alcoholic from spree spending on alcohol. As the alcoholic's life takes on more order and greater dimensions, the need for alcohol can be controlled to greater degrees.

## OTHER RESOURCES

The preceding discussion covered many areas in which the counselor may not have expertise, for example, the establishment of a monthly budget. The counselor may feel these are not appropriate concerns for counseling. When one considers the emotional impact and the influence on a client's drinking that such issues have, the appropriateness of their inclusion becomes clearer. Additionally, the counselor is often called on to meet a need that no other worker is available to meet. Counselors should be aware of consultants and resources in the community that may help the client. These include industry, vocational rehabilitation, local junior colleges, service groups, and government agencies. A prime example of commitment by such groups is the willingness of employers to contract with workers so that Antabuse is taken at work, thus ensuring the continued use of this drug as a deterrent to impulse drinking. Studies show that Antabuse works best when it is part of a contract based on an interpersonal relationship. Many bosses have committed themselves to such an involvement with new workers. *They, in return, would probably benefit from counselor praise for their efforts.*

Many clients do not consider themselves functioning until they can hold a job and do it well. The importance that it has to them is one incentive to the counselor's work in this area.

*Footnotes*

1. V. Dale and E. Walkstein. Vocational rehabilitation of patients on the Beth Israel Methadone Maintenance Program. *Mount Sinai Journal of Medicine,* 1974, *41* (1), 267-271.

2. R. Farber. *Handbook for the alcoholism counselor.* Baltimore: Alcoholism Center, Baltimore City Health Department, 1970.

# 10 Evaluating the Treatment Plan

## THE NEED FOR EVALUATION

The area of alcoholism treatment has become a dynamic, expanding one in which new methods are being developed to replace the punitive treatment of years ago. There is always a delay, however, between research and clinical application. Thus, those working with clients frequently find themselves left to their own resources in developing new treatment strategies. Often intuition is the basis for the treatment trial. If it seems to succeed with one client, the counselor is more apt to use it with others. Superstition or habit on the part of the counselor may become the major rationale for a treatment approach unless evaluation procedures are undertaken to substantiate the claim of treatment-related success.

Evaluation of the treatment plan is often omitted because its importance is not fully understood by either the client or the counselor. But systematic evaluation can be a rewarding and educational undertaking, and, at this stage of alcoholism rehabilitation, a necessary one for the advancement of the whole field.

The evaluation process can offer concrete proof that the therapeutic intervention has moved the client to a higher level of functioning in a specific behavioral area. Not only does such information help to build a general fund of treatment knowledge in the field but for the individual client and counselor it also becomes a reinforcer for making change, encouraging further work. The client begins to understand the control he has over his own behavior and therefore is less apt to blame hidden forces for setbacks in treatment. This is important, especially in dealing with alcoholic clients who have come to believe that alcohol consumption is totally out of their control.

The evaluation process also provides summary points in therapy and natural closure on treatment. The counselor and client determine the effectiveness of treatment, make changes, and agree on criteria for the attainment of goals in the unambiguous plan of the evaluation procedure.

Most often evaluation is conducted in an informal and idiosyncratic manner (e.g., the client "feels better" or "is doing better"). This leads to such problems as difference in goals and in criteria for change so that while one participant may feel that therapy has been successful, the other may be disappointed. Formalizing the evaluation procedure eliminates much of this by structuring criteria for success as an integral part of the treatment program. This consists of distinct procedures that easily can be taught to clients and staff (see Table 21).

---

*TABLE 21.   EVALUATION PROCEDURE*

*Assessment*

1. Gathering of baseline data (self-monitoring, observations, scales, written and behavioral tests)

2. Negotiation of treatment agreements for short- and long-term goals

*Treatment*

1. Initiation of treatment

2. Monitoring of treatment by client and others

3. Re-negotiation of goals, treatment, etc.

*Evaluation*

1. Gathering of post-treatment data

2. Comparison of pre- post- data

3. Evaluation of treatment benefits

4. Post-treatment suggestions to client; negotiation of additional therapeutic contracts, if necessary

---

## BASELINE DATA AND CONTINUOUS MONITORING

*Baseline data* offer specific information about the intensity, duration, or frequency of the target behavior. For example, client X drinks to intoxification only when he is home. Treatment could not be undertaken without careful information gathering on the antecedents to intoxification at home. Perhaps the client drinks to intoxification at home because (a) he is bored; (b) he does not get along with his family; (c) he has time to ruminate about a problem; (d) or some other reason. Specific information concerning thoughts, activities, and interactions will be necessary. Record and diary keeping enable clients and outside observers to collect such information. In Chapter 2 we described the procedure used to collect baseline data. Here we will briefly summarize that process.

The first step in data collection is a determination of *what* to collect. It is evident from our example that detailed initial interviewing will disclose the important contingencies on the target behaviors.

Next, *who* will collect the information and *how* it will be gathered must be outlined. Involving the client at the very onset gives him status as change agent and respected partner in the therapeutic team. The counselor, ward attendants, and family and friends are all potential participants in this endeavor. Having others collect the same data provides a *reliability check* showing whether the correct information is being gathered in the correct manner. Discrepancies indicate that some adjustment in data collection is needed.

The client should be given clear instructions and practice before being asked to collect information which will affect treatment. This can be accomplished in the counseling session. Client and counselor choose a behavior that can be observed by both participants, perhaps a verbal response (number of "uh's") or nonverbal one, such as the number of times the client touches his face. Each is given a card blocked in five one-minute slots, and each begins counting at exactly the same time. At the end of each minute, each will record the number of observations made. A comparison of the five slots will show how reliable the observers were in their observations. Such practice sessions will help clients become comfortable with observation and recording, and it will help show some practical problems of logistics. Clients seem to be more dependable about data collection when practice sessions have been given.

Recording observations continues into the treatment phase, serving as a guide and thus enabling adjustment of the program as the need arises. Such *ongoing monitoring* also serves to determine *when* a goal has been reached.

Discrete behaviors may be counted and charted easily, but there must first be agreement on *what* constitutes the behavior to be counted. For example, if degree of depression has been targeted, a clear definition must be agreed upon by participants. It will also be necessary to record information about the *antecedents* of depression. If we were simply to know the client reports depression in the evenings, we would still need to determine what occurs or does not occur then or prior to that time. Form 5 shows two examples of observation sheets which help structure record keeping.

*FORM 5.   SAMPLE RECORDING FORMS*

Name: _____

Behavior To Be Rated:          (For example, depression, sad-
                               ness, suicidal thoughts)

Scale:   1   2   3   4   5   6   7   8   9   10
         Least          Moderately          Most
         Intense        Intense             Intense

| Date | Time | Intensity | What were you doing? |
|------|------|-----------|----------------------|
|      |      |           |                      |
|      |      |           |                      |
|      |      |           |                      |

Name: _____

Behavior To Be Observed:

| Date | Time | Place | What occurred just before? | What occurred just after? |
|------|------|-------|----------------------------|---------------------------|
|      |      |       |                            |                           |
|      |      |       |                            |                           |
|      |      |       |                            |                           |

A handy guide in deciding the appropriate information to collect is the question, "What information is needed to meet the therapeutic goal?" For example, if the client complains of loneliness and desires to meet people, a check must be made on number of social approaches attempted and social skills possessed. A married couple who complains of financial difficulty should keep track of how they spend their paychecks.

Let us use this last problem as a larger example. The counselor asked the couple to record how they spent the last three months' earnings. They found there was a sizable amount which could not be accounted for, another amount which was spent on unnecessary items, and another amount which had been used for home and personal maintenance. After deliberation, the couple decided that the last amount, which was relatively stable from month to month, was an appropriate sum. The problem spending seemed clearly to be in the first two categories—unnecessary expenditures and unaccounted for expenditures. It was decided that they should keep daily accounts of expenditures and discuss these accounts at the end of each day. At the end of a two-week trial period, some change was noted, but they wished for a more immediate change, especially in spending for unnecessary items. They decided that reinforcement would speed improvement, so they instituted a system whereby a small monetary reward was given at the end of each day in which they stayed within their budget. Building in a small amount of money which did not have to be justified seemed to be the necessary motivator in this instance. The couple saw a satisfactory change in the account keeping. They received additional reinforcement by finding they were within their budget for the month and by discovering that bill paying had become less aversive. They also found they were having fewer arguments and attributed this to the alleviation of financial worries.

Charting alone is sometimes so reinforcing to clients that other reinforcers are not necessary. In the above example, there was some change when a systematic method of problem solving and recording of change was introduced. Often, however, allowing for suitable reinforcers will speed change or allow clients to continue a program over a long period.

Figure 3 is a descriptive summary of the information collected by the couple. A three-month baseline (collected retrospectively) was considered adequate since the percentage spent in each area remained relatively *stable*. That is, little fluctuation was noted in spending over the three months. Had there been a great fluctuation (for example, in unaccounted for spending: January = 20%; February = 12%; March =

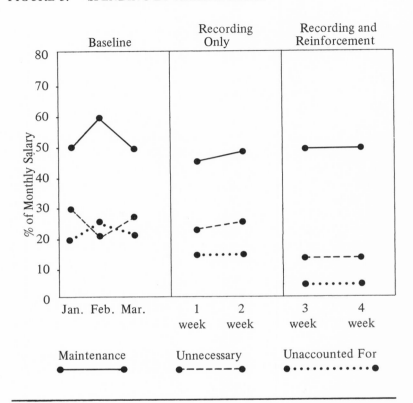

FIGURE 3.    SPENDING BY JIM AND MARY

40%), it might have been necessary to collect more data over a greater number of months. Obtaining stable baseline data is an especially important point when one considers target behaviors, such as alcohol consumed, degree of depression, and kind of interactions with one's partner. If the baseline is not stable, we cannot say we have an accurate picture of the target behavior. It takes patience to postpone treatment until enough baseline data are collected, but treatment cannot be adequately planned without complete information.

In the example of the couple, recording the amount of daily expenditures was helpful. The points in the recording phase represent percentage of the week's income which was spent in each area. The graph shows that the two were able to change their spending habits. The daily monitoring enabled them to pinpoint problem areas. Excerpts from the couple's daily record follow:

168

5 April
John
12:00—Lunch—$2.50
12:45—Drug Store—$3.88 (shaving cream—$1.59; magazine, $1.50; cigarette lighter on impulse, $.79)

Mary
12:00—Lunch—0.00 (sandwich and fruit from home)
12:30—Clothing store—$40.00 (purse on impulse, $32.00; birthday gift, $8.00)

A check on the type of spending allowed the couple to build in safeguards to spending. The lunch-time impulse spending was seen as a daily problem for John, often adding up to $15 or more, weekly. Although Mary did not shop at noon often, when she did, she was likely to spend a large sum. They both decided that they would avoid noon-time shopping and if unavoidable, they would list ahead of time what they needed and the approximate price. They would then carry only that sum, leaving extra money, checks, and credit cards locked in their office drawers. Graphing alone would not have given the couple the information to develop the strategy to avoid noon-time spending.

## PRE-POST TREATMENT COMPARISONS
A growing number of alcoholism workers are using pre-post measures to determine the effectiveness of treatment. A discussion of self-reports, the filling out of questionnaires, and reports from others is provided in Chapter 2. These may be given before and after treatment and compared for approximate changes. Examples of the use of such measures follow.

### Example A
Lou B. is an inpatient who was being prepared for discharge. During one phase of assessment, she had been asked to fill out the Reinforcement Survey Schedule and the Fear Inventory. Now that discharge was imminent, a closer analysis of these two self-reports was made. It was found that reinforcers were few and consisted of solitary activities and consumption of food and beverages. Fears were pervasive. It was felt that a broader range of reinforcers and a lessening of the reported fears must be accomplished for Lou to have success outside the hospital. Treatment consisted of introducing her to possible classes of reinforcers, especially those that would have her interact with others. Fears were treated in a variety of ways: some dissipated when correct information was given; some were treated by gradual real or imaginary

desensitization. A pre-post comparison was then made by administering the inventories to Lou. It was found that reinforcers had developed and fears had dissipated or were under control. The chance of success after hospitalization was raised considerably by this phase of treatment.

## Example B

Assessment revealed that the client, Joe B., had lost (a) a series of jobs when he became angry at his supervisor for directing his actions; (b) was separated from his wife because of his bursts of anger at home; (c) drank when he felt others had taken advantage of him, and (d) experienced physiological symptoms of anxiety when interacting with adults.

Treatment consisted of social-skills training in which Joe learned to control his anger, discuss problems with his superiors and peers, and make his wishes known; training in anxiety-alleviating techniques; and self-management training in which he learned to drink only in prearranged ways (e.g., he agreed not to drink when angry, anxious, or depressed).

At the end of treatment, the client and counselor reviewed assessment data, comparing them with the results of treatment. Joe had been working, so during treatment, potential or actual work problems were handled. Success could then be measured by time on the job and also by the number of potential problems avoided and actual ones resolved. Time on the job meant number of days worked per month verified by the client's pay stub. To assess the client's ability to solve work problems, the counselor asked Joe to re-enact a problem interaction including the response of the other workers involved. In this way, the counselor could determine how effective social-skills training had been.

Joe's wife had agreed to see him and reported a change in his behavior. By the wife's report, her agreement to become involved in treatment was directly related to the changes she perceived in her husband. She also verified Joe's ability to drink in the prearranged manner. When he did slip (gulping drinks or drinking more than had been planned), he was able to remove himself from the situation before he became intoxicated.

## THE SINGLE-CASE STUDY

The single-case study is a basic experimental method conducted by collecting baseline information on the behavior of interest. When this baseline has stabilized, the treatment procedure is instituted on the particular behavior until change occurs. A comparison of change with baseline data will show the effectiveness of treatment. Such a procedure ensures that change is due to the treatment used; this may be demonstrated by removing the treatment and allowing the behavior to return to baseline strength. Of course, treatment would be instituted again to affect needed change.

The single-case study offers control over treatment procedures. By using a treatment procedure in a planned manner, one is more confident that changes are not due to extraneous factors but indeed may be attributed to the therapeutic intervention and can be expected to occur again, given the same conditions.

Counselors using the single-case design find this an efficient, unobtrusive way to evaluate treatment outcome and effectiveness of procedure (see Table 22).

---

*TABLE 22.    SINGLE-CASE STUDY*

1. Background of problem
   a. general background
   b. specific patient background
2. Method to be followed
   a. assessment of problem
   b. gathering of baseline data
   c. selection of target behaviors
   d. development of treatment strategy
   e. on-going monitoring
3. Analysis of results
4. Post-Assessment
   a. comparison of pre- and post-tests
   b. interpretation of results

---

## Example Of A Single-Case Study

*Background:* This is a rationale for treatment and is usually based on past publications as well as the counselor's clinical experience.

*General Background:* Alcohol is often used to relieve anxiety, mask inadequacies, self-medicate, etc. That is, an individual may find he receives some relief of stress by alcohol consumption. Although the relief is short-lived and, over time induces other problems, the individual is not often deterred by this logic.

*Specific Background:* The client history specific to the problem under consideration is outlined.

Mr. H. used alcohol to relieve low back pain which resulted from a work accident. Surgery was performed a number of years ago, and the only remaining outward sign of his injury was a slow, uneven gait in which he favored his right leg. The client had complained of pain of varying intensity since the accident and surgery. All consultants were in agreement that the pain would continue throughout the client's life.

Mr. H. had sharply curtailed his activities. He no longer worked, spending most of his day with a group of men who were also unemployed. His marriage, which had been good, showed the strain of the crisis. Mrs. H. reported her husband was short-tempered, quick to punish their children, and spent little time in the company of his family.

Always a heavy beer drinker, Mr. H. began to spend much of his time intoxicated, stating that the pain was more bearable.

*Assessment:* Based on history, observation, and tests, the client's problems are outlined.

During assessment the client, his wife, and his counselor agreed that increased alcohol consumption was directly related to Mr. H.'s preception of pain and that attention to pain and attempts at relief interfered with his daily life to a serious degree. Associated problems included inability to make appropriate interpersonal, vocational, and physical adjustments in his lifestyle.

*Baseline Information:* This is a record showing the extent of the problem before treatment.

Mr. H. was asked to (a) record pain intensity over a two-week period before treatment began, using a sheet similar to Form 1 (shown earlier); (b) keep a daily activity log (Table 23); and (c) keep a record of beer consumed.

*Target Behaviors:* A working definition of target behaviors is necessary. Unless everyone involved in treatment understands what the target behavior consists of, unreliable information will be collected.

In this case the target behaviors were identified as (1) intensity of pain and (2) amount of beer consumed.

It was felt that as the target behaviors decreased, the client would increase acceptable behaviors (that is, make appropriate readjustment in interpersonal, vocational, and physical areas).

*Treatment:* This consists of a complete treatment plan.

Records indicated that consumption of beer was related to perceived intensity of pain (Figure 4). Mr. H.'s daily schedule showed a deprived life centered about the alleviation of pain. It was decided that treatment would consist of (a) gradual rearrangement of his daily schedule so that a refocusing of attention might be accomplished; (b)

172

TABLE 23.    MR. H.'s DAILY LOG, SUMMARIZED*

| | |
|---|---|
| 9 a.m. | Awake |
| 10 a.m. | Dress |
| 11 a.m.-4 p.m. | Meet friends at bar |
| 5 p.m. | Return home for dinner |
| 6 p.m. | Watch TV or go out |
| 1 a.m. | Retire |

*Each day was similar.

continuation of self-monitoring of pain intensity, beer consumption, and daily activities (Mrs. H. was encouraged to verbally reinforce the client for involving himself in activities.); and (c) complete discussion of intractable pain in which it was agreed that pain was present and that a certain degree would have to be tolerated. The client agreed that he had curtailed his activities to an unnecessary degree and that when he was active the pain was more tolerable.

*Post-Assessment:* Evaluation of change from pre- to post-treatment is made by comparison of data.

FIGURE 4.    RECORD OF MR. H.'s DRINKING

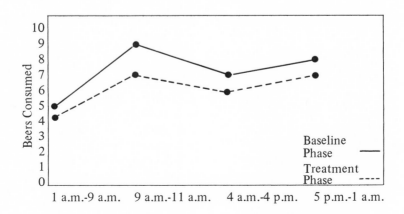

Evaluation of treatment outcome consisted of a comparison of baseline and post-treatment data (degree of pain reported, amount of beer consumed, daily activities, self-reports, and spouse reports). Figure 4 shows that the client's drinking continued to decrease during treatment. Mr. H.'s records show that level of perceived pain remained approximately the same during treatment when activities were increased as when alcohol was used to mask pain. The client reported that seeing the graph convinced him as nothing else had that he could function again.

## EXPERIMENTAL DESIGNS

Experimental designs offer the opportunity to test treatment techniques and assumption in a formalized manner.

Three designs or procedures follow: the *reversal* design, (or *ABAB design*), the *multiple baseline* design, and the *control group* design. These designs are presented in the expectation that, once the counselor learns the effectiveness of evaluation, he will wish to use more experimental procedures to accomplish it. In addition, programs funded by federal monies are expected to show verifiable change in their clientele. The following designs, especially the control group design, will accomplish this.

### Reversal Design (ABAB)

The **reversal**, or **ABAB design**, alternates the baseline phase (A) and treatment phase (B) to demonstrate that a functional relationship exists between the target behavior and the treatment. This relationship is shown to exist when a systematic change in the occurrence of the behavior can be demonstrated by the presentation and removal of the treatment.

The baseline phase (A) continues until a stable response rate is obtained or until it is obvious that the target behavior will not improve over time. This phase serves as a comparison for the evaluation of change attributed to the treatment program. A baseline phase of several days is usually allotted.

Treatment, phase (B), is next instituted and continues until behavior reaches a stable level or displays a change from baseline. *Return to baseline* (A) (or, in other terms, the *reversal phase*) is introduced. That is, treatment is discontinued and the conditions of baseline are allowed to recur unimpeded by intervention. This is a necessary stage to determine whether the treatment was indeed responsible for the change in behavior. If behavior reverts to approximate baseline rate, we can be confident that change during phase (B) is functionally related to treatment and not simply a chance occurrence.

Finally, treatment (B) is reinstated, and change in behavior from baseline is observed. The increase over baseline in the two treatment phases allows confidence that the treatment program caused change in the target behavior. In the example shown in Figure 5, the client's negative self-statements prevented her from successfully engaging in social situations.

Using the Premack Principle, Ms. S. was asked to pair a low probability behavior (positive statements about herself) with a high probability behavior (coffee drinking).

There are instances, however, when it is impractical or undesirable to use a reversal design. Clients who reduce or stop heavy drinking would not be asked to resume drinking. Likewise, couples near divorce may not be able to tolerate a reversal phase, and a new boss may not allow a client to resume aggressive behavior or miss work days for sake of an experimental design. Even when consequences are not so aversive, it is often discouraging to make behavior worsen even for a short time. Other designs can be implemented to demonstrate program effects. For example, multiple baseline designs can be used.

## Multiple Baseline Design

Baseline data are often obtained simultaneously for several behaviors. In the **multiple baseline design**, treatment is implemented for *one* target behavior while baseline data collection continues for the other behaviors. In this way, behavior change is shown to be associated with treatment instead of chance occurrence. When data rates are stable for all target behaviors, a second target behavior is introduced into treatment. It is expected that base rate for each behavior will remain constant *until* treatment is introduced.

Multiple baseline design demonstrates effects by introducing treatment over time, thus making the reversal phase unnecessary. Because the baseline behaviors continue at a stable rate (that is, they do not change as treatment is introduced for one target behavior), we can say that a functional relationship occurs between the treatment and the target behavior.

However, change must occur only in the behavior targeted and not in those still in baseline. Therefore, appropriateness of this design must be questioned if generalization is likely to occur. For example, change in one individual, especially those living or working closely together, may cause other individuals to change. Likewise, change may generalize to other behaviors or situations targeted in the design. Nevertheless, the design is a good one, given this precaution.

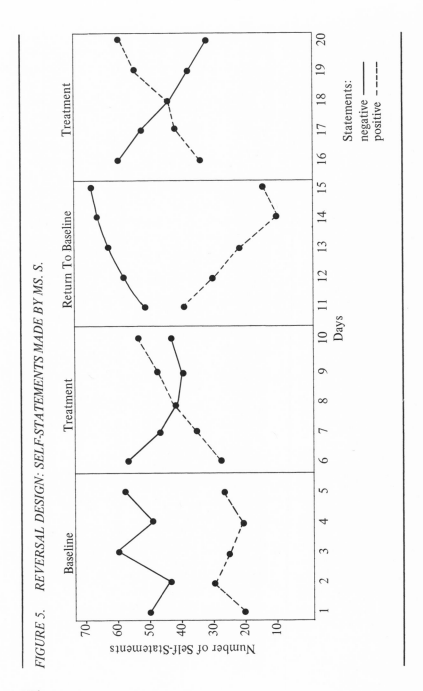

FIGURE 5.  REVERSAL DESIGN: SELF-STATEMENTS MADE BY MS. S.

An example of multiple baseline design is shown in Figure 6. The client wished to spend more time with his family but found it aversive since he expected to be rejected by them. Baseline consisted of time spent interacting with his wife and his two children. After baseline data were collected, treatment was instituted with increase in time spent with his wife targeted for change. When that treatment phase stabilized, time spent with his older child was included in the treatment. Lastly, time with his younger child was brought under the treatment program. Treatment consisted of the counselor's and client's practicing interactions including responses to ward off rejection.

In a similar manner, multiple baseline design may be used across individuals and across situations. In the earlier examples, behaviors were introduced individually into treatment. Individuals or situations are introduced one at a time when the multiple baseline design is used *across individuals* and *across situations.* For example, on a ward where clients are not participating in group therapy, the counselor first obtains base rates on all individuals. This may be a quick check of times each has attended group sessions during the past several weeks. Then one person is selected for individual attention prior to the group meeting. When behavior rate is stabilized (that is, individual A shows steady rate of change from baseline attendance whereas other group participants continue to show base rate behavior), individual B is included in treatment. This procedure continues until all participants are included in the treatment.

This is a useful design when a particular behavior change is desired for a group, such as inpatient units, outpatient groups, families, and work groups.

An example of multiple-baseline design *across situations* is one in which client M. drinks in anxiety-inducing situations. Five discrete situations are identified with their particular, but similar, reasons for anxiety production. He drinks in the evenings when (1) his supervisor has indicated his performance on the assembly line is too slow, (2) his co-workers have left him out of noontime conversations, (3) his wife confronts him with household budget problems, (4) he argues with his teenage son, and (5) he has to compete on the office bowling team with players more skilled than he is. Baseline data are obtained for each situation and treatment instituted for one. In a manner similar to the examples of multiple baseline design used across individuals, each of Mr. M.'s anxiety producing situations would be successively brought under treatment.

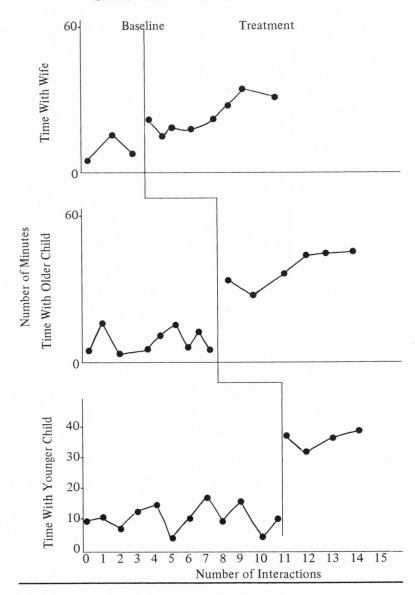

FIGURE 6.  *MULTIPLE BASELINE DESIGN
SHOWING CHANGE IN TIME
SPENT WITH FAMILY MEMBERS*

## Control Group Design

A design which uses a randomized* control** group is often referred to as a true experimental design. The simplest study calls for two groups, the **experimental** (treatment) **group** and the **control** (nontreatment) **group**. The procedure for the control group design is summarized below:

1. Randomly select subjects, assign to group, and designate experimental and control groups.
2. Pre-test groups on the variable in question (called the *dependent variable*).
3. Obtain mean score for each group.
4. Apply the treatment condition (*independent variable*) to the treatment group only, being certain that both groups are treated the same otherwise.
5. Post-test both of the groups using an equal adaptation of the pre-test.
6. Obtain mean score for each group.
7. Obtain the difference between the pre- and post-test mean scores (X pre—X post = X).
8. Compare the differences (X treatment group and X control group) and determine if the two groups differ in terms of the treatment given.
9. Use appropriate statistical tests to determine if a significant difference exists.

For those interested in using the control group experiments, references of some excellent handbooks have been included at the end of this chapter.

## SPECIAL PROBLEMS

There are certain practical problems encountered in evaluating treatment effectiveness, but they should not deter one from implementing evaluation procedures. In fact, attention paid to these issues makes for better outcome evaluation.

---

*randomized:* Clients are assigned to one of two or more treatment groups randomly; that is, each client has an equal chance of being assigned to any treatment group. The easiest method to use is assigning clients successively to treatment groups as they enter the treatment program. Randomization insures that all extraneous variables or characteristics are spread throughout the groups as chance occurrences.

**control group:* The control group is given the exact kind of treatment as the experimental group *except* for the one condition which is under study.

## Follow-up Data

After the treatment has terminated, the counselor may wish to contact the client for follow-up information. It is useful to include this in the initial contract set during the assessment period. In this way, the client is aware that the follow-up effort will be made and is more amenable to participation.

Follow-up data are useful in several ways. They allow additional evaluation of treatment over time, indicating whether *"booster" treatments* are needed. Data may also be collected to determine whether the client is able to use the principles of treatment in other situations. This is important since therapists who use behavioral techniques place a certain amount of value on teaching their clients, thus giving them control over their behavior. For example, a client who learned to control impulsive responses in work situations now finds that she can handle social situations better, too. Upon questioning, the client describes using techniques that were taught in the counseling sessions.

Follow-up is best if preplanned to obtain specific information. It may take the form of personal interview. However, in many areas this is inconvenient because the distance the client must travel is great. Telephone or mail contact may be more practical.

A model follow-up system might include interview, standardized testing, and behavioral observation.

The interview consists of a standardized form to assist the counselor in obtaining information specifically about the client's drinking problem. For example, the counselor would want to know if an abstainer had found it exceptionally difficult to abstain, had experienced any slip-ups, or had found particular situations troublesome; about controlled drinkers, the counselor would inquire whether any change in drinking from the prescribed manner had occurred and whether any adjustments were needed. The counselor would also evaluate the client's other special problems (e.g., work, marital, self-image, the areas targeted for treatment at the time of assessment plus those that were later included).

The counselor might re-administer the standardized tests which were given the client during pre- and post-assessment. Such tests as the Beck Depression Inventory[1] and the Wolpe-Lazarus Assertiveness Test[2] are quickly administered and scored.

Using behavioral observations and test situations similar to those used to assess such behaviors as social skills provides a more accurate assessment than using self-report alone. This combination gives the counselor a good idea of how well the client has incorporated new adaptive behaviors into her repertoire of skills. With access to video or audio equipment, the counselor can put the client into problem situations and assess the appropriateness of her response. In addition to evaluation, this procedure will assist in determining what areas need booster treatments.

For example, Ms. J. had had difficulty refusing drinks at luncheon work meetings and business parties. A program of anticipating problem situations, refusal practice, development of avoidance tactics, and reinforcement for coping was instituted. Results were excellent. Upon follow-up, Ms. J. presented a record of business contacts in which alcohol was present and a record of her handling of the problem. In addition, she was asked to handle simulated situations so that the counselor might determine Ms. J.'s effectiveness. A positive correlation between Ms. J.'s recording and her handling of the simulated situations allowed a more confident estimation of her success. Had there been a discrepancy, the counselor might have checked further and considered some intensive retraining or refresher sessions.

In addition, the client may use this time to consult the counselor about other concerns. In this way, follow-up becomes a means of dealing with problems before they reach crisis proportion. Too, clients will be more receptive to follow-up if they receive something that is of immediate benefit.

It is customary to have a follow-up appointment soon after discharge of an inpatient. Two weeks to one month is usual. There seems to be less stress on follow-up when the client has been treated as an outpatient. It may be that the transition to nonclient status is not so apparent with outpatients. Such clients have been maintaining themselves in a home, probably with a family and a job, so termination of counseling sessions seems not as important, given the client's complete life situation. However, the importance to the client should not be underestimated. The counselor has become a reliable source of reinforcement. If this source is taken away suddenly, the client may have difficulty shifting to others who might give reinforcement.

We cannot feel full confidence that treatment has been successful unless the client can maintain gains over several months. Complete evaluation will consist of follow-up evaluation of at least one year's duration.

## Behavioral Observations

Those using behavioral intervention rely greatly on observation in naturalistic settings. It is assumed that this will be more reliable and more useful than retrospective reports.

Essentially, this is so. However, we are becoming aware that problems also exist with this method. In the following paragraphs we discuss the most apparent problems and offer suggestions in dealing with them.

## Client Cooperation

Self-monitoring is an integral part of any treatment with alcoholic clients. Number of drinks, thoughts about drinking, self-derogatory thoughts, nonassertive behaviors, explosive responses, physiological indices of anxiety, interpersonal interactions are examples of the wide variety of behaviors the patient might be asked to monitor.

Eliciting cooperation from clients requires that they be educated to the purpose as well as technique of recording. The use of concrete examples to demonstrate procedure and rationale is essential. Having practice sessions, eliciting questions, and anticipating difficulties are also necessary.

It should be clear that monitoring is a step in the process of attaining the goals set by the client and an on-going check that treatment is progressing as planned. The procedure should be made as nonintrusive on the client's life as possible. Not only should the recording consume little time (for example, behavior-counting is quicker than diary-keeping), but it also should be inconspicuous to others.

A word might be said about reinforcement in connection with self-monitoring. Self-monitoring itself is usually rewarding for the client in that change may be seen, enhancing incentive to continue with the program.

The counselor may reinforce the client's efforts in recording. Likewise, reinforcement may be withheld in the form of shortened sessions or no sessions if the client has not monitored target behaviors. This is best discussed beforehand and included in the initial contract.

## Footnotes

1. A. T. Beck, C. H. Ward, M. Mendelson, J. Mock, and J. Erbaugh. An inventory for measuring depression. *Archives of General Psychiatry,* 1961, *4,* 561-571.

2. J. Wolpe and A. Lazarus. *Behavior therapy techniques.* New York: Pergamon Press, Inc., 1966.

*Reading List On Control Group Experiments*

Anderson, Barry F. *The psychology experiment, an introduction to the scientific method.* Belmont, CA: Wadsworth Publishing Co., Inc., 1966.

Campbell, Donald T., and Stanley, Julian C. *Experimental and quasi-experimental designs for research.* Chicago: Rand McNally College Publishing Co., 1963.

Isaac, Stephen, and Michael, William B. *Handbook in research and evaluation.* San Diego: Robert R. Knapp, Publisher, 1971.

# Technical Glossary

*Affect.* Emotional expression.

*Alpha-wave conditioning.* Training to increase alpha brain-wave production by indicating to the individual when alpha waves are present on an electroencephalograph (EEG); used for such purposes as pain control and tension release.

*Analogue.* Similar to a real-life situation; a simulation of.

*Antabuse.* Trade name for the medication, *disulfiram,* which when taken daily will interact with ingested alcohol to cause such symptoms as nausea, vomiting, sweating, heart palpitations, and low-blood pressure.

*Antecedent event.* Any single event or set of circumstances that occurs immediately prior to a behavioral response.

*Anxiety.* A vague feeling of apprehension and fear.

*Approximation procedure.* Method in which the end goal is reached by accomplishing components of it in a systematic, stepwise fashion. For example, the end goal of orgasm with a partner may be reached by approximating that goal; that is, the individual may learn to orgasm through (a) self-stimulation, (b) self-stimulation and fantasy of the partner, (c) manual stimulation jointly by self and partner, (d) manual stimulation by partner, and (e) coitus with partner to orgasm.

*Assertion training.* A therapeutic procedure in which an individual is taught to express personal rights and feelings, usually by means of specific instructions, examples, practice, feedback, and reward.

*Assertiveness.* The appropriate expression of personal rights and feelings (both positive and negative).

*Aversion therapy.* A therapeutic procedure which attempts to inhibit an undesirable behavior or response by repeatedly associating that behavior with an unpleasant or noxious event, such as electrical shock or nausea-producing drugs.

*Behavioral asset.* A special positive behavioral attribute that helps an individual adjust to life.

*Behavioral deficit.* A behavior which is considered to be a problem because it occurs too infrequently, not intensely enough, or for too short a period of time (e.g., impotence).

*Behavioral excess.* A behavior which is considered to be a problem because it occurs too frequently, too intensely, or for too long a period of time (e.g., explosive outbursts of anger).

*Chromatography.* A process of identifying solutions or chemical compounds, which is frequently used to analyze a breath sample for a blood/alcohol level determination.

*Clitoris.* In the female, a small elongated mass of tissue situated along the anterior surface and midline to the vulva, homologous to the penis in the male; its purpose is strictly limited to the reception and transmittal of sexual tension.

*Coitus.* Sexual intercourse between a male and a female.

*Complaintant.* The client or patient who identifies a situation or behavior as being problematic. For example, the father (complaintant) identifies his son's late hours as disruptive to their relationship; the wife (complaintant) cannot reach orgasm because her husband is a premature ejaculator.

*Consequent event.* Any single event or set of circumstances that occurs immediately after a behavioral response.

*Continuum.* A succession along a continuous dimension as opposed to being expressed in discrete categories.

*Contraindicated.* Considered inadvisable.

*Coronal ridge.* The ridge which surrounds the base of the penis.

*Covert conditioning.* A process that can be used either to increase or decrease the occurrence of a thought by having the individual repeatedly associate a thought of the desirable behavior with a positive or rewarding thought or pairing the undesirable behavior with a punishing thought, respectively.

*Covert sensitization.* A process in which cues targeted for change are repeatedly associated with unpleasant experiences and images.

*Cue.* A specific stimulus event which, because of past associations, serves to trigger a behavior pattern.

*Delirum tremens.* A severe form of alcohol withdrawal occurring after termination of heavy drinking, which is associated with sweating, agitation, heart palpitations, and convulsions.

*Depression.* A marked feeling of despondency and sadness associated with an inability to concentrate, lack of energy, crying, guilt feelings, early morning awakening, decreased appetite, and decreased sexual desire.

*Detoxification.* The process of "drying out" an alcoholic.

*Disulfiram. See* Antabuse.

*Dysfunction.* An impairment; abnormal functioning.

*Ejaculation.* The process in which semen is suddenly and forcibly discharged by the penis during the male's orgasm.

*Electromyogram (EMG).* The record of electrical activity in muscles, monitored via the attachment of electrodes to the muscles under study.

*Electromyography.* The study of electrical activity in muscles.

*Endometriosis.* A condition in which uterine mucous membrane occurs in parts of the pelvic cavity where it is not normally present and may result in unusual menses, sterility, dyspareunia.

*Etiology.* Cause.

*Extinction.* A process by which the probability of occurrence of a behavior is decreased by withholding reinforcers for that behavior.

*Facilitative.* Contributing to problem-solving. Facilitative behaviors encourage positive interaction between people. Facilitative statements include suggested solutions, acceptance of responsibility, willingness to compromise.

*Female dispareunia.* Painful or difficult coitus which results from vaginismus, infection, lesions or abnormalities of the female genital tract, inadequate lubrication.

*Frenulum.* The fold of skin on the coronal ridge which is on the lower surface of the penis.

*Functional behavioral analysis.* Describing a behavior pattern in terms of its relationship to antecedent and consequent events.

*Functional therapeutic system.* A therapeutic plan based on modifying the antecedents and consequences of a behavior pattern.

*Hallucinate.* To perceive falsely, i.e., to see, hear, touch, or smell something that does not exist in reality.

*Heart palpitations.* A rapid heart beat which is often associated with a stress situation.

*Impotence.* Inability to attain or sustain an erection to the completion of coitus or to the satisfaction of both the male and his partner.

*Impotence, primary.* Disturbance in which the male has never been able to attain or sustain an erection sufficient to complete coitus or to the satisfaction of both partners.

*Impotence, secondary.* Disturbance in which the male is unable to attain or sustain an erection to complete coitus to the satisfaction of both partners, after a history of satisfactory erections.

*Independent variables.* Stimulus events which influence a behavioral response (e.g., method of treatment).

*Maintaining factor.* Any one or a combination of social, situational, emotional, cognitive, and physiological events, currently existing, which serves to insure the continued occurrence of a behavior pattern.

*Masturbatory fantasy.* Sex imagery during self-stimulation used by the individual to accomplish orgasm.

*Milieu therapy.* A therapeutic procedure in which the total social environment becomes influential in the treatment process; often accompanied by self-government by patients in an inpatient setting.

*Modality.* A therapeutic technique or treatment.

*Modeling.* Technique in which desired behavior is demonstrated for the client to observe; modeling is often used as one method in social-skills training.

*Monilia.* (also called monoliasis and candidiasis). A common infection of the mucosa; when seen in the vagina, accompanied by a discharge and inflammation of the vaginal walls with possible painful coitus resulting.

*Nonfacilitative.* Not contributing to problem solving. Nonfacilitative statements which hinder problem solving include criticisms, interruptions, and complaints.

*"Oral" dependency.* A psychoanalytic concept which implies that problem drinking is an expression of the alcoholic's unmet dependency needs during the oral stage of psychological development.

*Orgasm.* The point of climax of sexual excitement, which usually occurs toward the end of coitus.

*Perineum.* The area of tissue between the thighs which extends from the posterior wall of the vagina in the female, and from the scrotum in the male, to the anus.

*Phobia.* An intense, debilitating and unreasonable fear which causes a curtailment in one's activity and an increase in avoidance behavior. One may become phobic to persons, places, things, or ideas; i.e., phobic fear of water, or a certain group of people, or the dark.

*Placebo effects.* Effects which occur because of the attention and suggestion the individual associates with a certain procedure (change associated with suggestion rather than with given treatment).

*Placebo factors.* Factors which result in improvements in behavior more as a function of suggestion and expectation than specific therapeutic influences.

*Precipitant.* Any single event or set of circumstances which serves as a stimulus for the occurrence of a behavior pattern.

*Precipitating factor.* Any one or a combination of social, situational, emotional, cognitive, and physiological events, which originally brought about the occurrence of a behavior pattern but which does not necessarily exist or influence the behavior at the present time.

*Premack Principle.* A phenomenon in which a high probability behavior (i.e., one which occurs frequently) can be used to reinforce (i.e., increase the likelihood of occurrence) a low probability behavior (i.e., one which occurs infrequently).

*Psychodrama.* A therapeutic procedure during which patients act out problems and conflicts in role-played interpersonal encounters simulating real-life interactions.

*Psychophysiological.* Pertaining to a disorder of the body which is caused by or associated with the emotions (e.g., peptic ulcers).

*Quantifying.* Describing a behavior pattern numerically in such terms as frequency of occurrence, rate, intensity, etc.

*Rational emotive therapy.* A psychological treatment system based on the assumption that adjustment problems arise from irrational patterns of thinking related to an individual's basic belief system.

*Reciprocity counseling.* Procedure based on each partner's giving reinforcement only when the other partner also is giving reinforcement or pleasure. The goal of this type of marital counseling is to maximize the number and kind of positive interactions partners give and receive.

*Relaxation training.* A therapeutic procedure in which an individual is taught deep muscular and mental relaxation.

*Sensate focus.* A technique used in sex therapy in which the couple learns to enjoy each other's pleasurable touching in a nonsexual way and without assuming that it commits them to coitus.

*Sex-steroid replacement therapy.* Hormonal therapy used in older males and females, which may aid in attaining greater sexual satisfaction for them.

*Shaping.* Teaching a behavior pattern through reinforcing small, successive steps until the final behavior occurs.

*Significant other.* An individual with whom one has a close, personal relationship, such as a relative or a friend.

*Systematic desensitization.* A therapeutic procedure used to treat specific unrealistic fears (i.e., phobias), in which deep muscular relaxation is repeatedly associated with thoughts of the feared object, person, or situation.

*Tolerance.* A condition that occurs with chronic heavy use of alcohol, in which increasingly more alcohol must be ingested to achieve the same "high" that lower doses previously would produce.

*Transactional analysis.* A therapeutic system in which the therapist helps an individual recognize and cope with his involvement in interpersonal "games" which result in adjustment problems.

*Vaginal containment.* The holding of the penis by the vagina.

*Vaginismus.* A psychophysiological disorder in which the muscles of the outer third of the vagina involuntarily contract because of imagined, anticipated, or actual attempt to enter the vagina, thus preventing completion of coitus.

*Visual acuity.* The ability of the eye to adjust to visual detail and bring it into focus.